"Pam Kanaly draws on her years of experience in single-parent ministry, showing us how to raise successful children alone. If you want to master the negative emotional roadblocks of single motherhood instead of them being the master over you, take time to read this book."

—Dr. Joe White, president and owner of Kanakuk Kamps

"Pam Kanaly is a firecracker with an obvious passion to set women free with the message of Jesus Christ. This book is certain to enlighten, encourage, and refresh single mothers who need God's answers in how to overcome negative emotions."

—Jennifer Maggio, author and founder of the
Life of a Single Mom Ministries

"In this book, Pam Kanaly meets you right where you are, encouraging your next step on the single-parenting journey. With compassion and wisdom, she equips you to handle this unique rollercoaster ride with hope and strength. If you buy one book this year, make it this one."

—Elsa Kok Colopy, former editor of *Single Parent Family* for Focus on the Family and author of
The Single Mom's Guide to Keeping It All Together

"Wow! What an awesome, real, raw, and heartfelt book. Pam Kanaly does a wonderful job of sharing practical and biblical truths that will change your perspective of being a single parent. This book ministers deeply to the pressing needs of single mothers. It's a must-read."

—Herbert Cooper, senior pastor,
People's Church, Oklahoma City

D1114100

The Single Mom and Her Rollercoaster Emotions

East Baton Rouge Parish Library
Baton Rouge, Louisiana

The Single Mom and Her Rollercoaster Emotions

By Pam Kanaly

PELICAN PUBLISHING COMPANY
GRETNA 2014

The word "Pelican" and the depiction of a pelican are
trademarks of Pelican Publishing Company, Inc., and are
registered in the U.S. Patent and Trademark Office.

Library of Congress Cataloging-in-Publication Data

Kanaly, Pam.
  The single mom and her rollercoaster emotions / by Pam Kanaly.
    pages cm
  Includes bibliographical references.
  ISBN 978-1-4556-1861-3 (pbk. : alk. paper) — ISBN 978-1-4556-
1862-0 (e-book) 1. Single mothers. 2. Parenting—Religious aspects.
I. Title.
  HQ759.915.K365 2014
  306.874'32--dc23

                                        2013041298

All Scripture quotations are taken from the *New American Standard
Bible.* Copyright © 1960, 1962, 1963, 1968, 1971, 1972, 1973, 1975,
1977 by The Lockman Foundation. Used by permission.

Printed in the United States of America

Published by Pelican Publishing Company, Inc.
1000 Burmaster Street, Gretna, Louisiana 70053

To my two children, Jason Scarbrough and Sara Maulsby. I dedicate this labor of love to you. Your lives are proof that children can and do emerge out of single-parent homes as men and women who love Christ with all their hearts, souls, minds, and strength. I pray that God's blessings continue to abound upon you, your spouses, and children. I thank God for the lessons of life we learned together.

I love you bunches,
Mom

Contents

Introduction

Rollercoasters—you either love them or you don't. As for me, just watching one race toward its destination makes me dizzy. I would venture to say that, as a single mom, you don't care for them either. They remind you all too well of your plight in raising children alone. One minute you're on a peak—*Yes, Lord, I can do this*—while the next minute you encounter the nauseating plunge—*No, Lord, I can't do this after all!* Being on a rollercoaster promises one thing: unpredictable ups and downs, similar to your runaway emotions as you handle your single-motherhood role.

Emotions are crazy and mysterious. Have you noticed? They drive, challenge, and control you. Emotions have a mind of their own. They fluctuate, flare up, bless, or depress. They are convincing, fickle, satisfying, confusing, unruly, dangerous, and oftentimes exhilarating. They can be your best friends, granting expansive pleasure from what's happening on the inside, or they can be your worst foes, signaling extensive danger from what's happening on the outside.

Because God is an emotional God, He's given us emotions, too. But what happens when we're stuck in how we feel and can't change? How can we learn to manage our emotions so that they don't manage us? Where is the control switch to bring this crazy carnival ride to a halt long enough to get our bearings as a parent? Why can't we move past debilitating thoughts that hamper productive parenting and spiritual growth? After all, we parent all day long, so why can't we "parent" our emotions?

Friends, it is my desire that you come to know the healing power of Jesus Christ and His heart in setting you free. God has given you His Holy Spirit, your life navigator, to come alongside to restore your past, empower your present, and foster your future. God is for you!

Single moms carry the hardest job in the entire world. No one masters the craft of being a juggler quite like you. You're the cook, moneymaker, spiritual leader, taxi driver, homework monitor, and more. You give and give and give, having no time for yourself. But what about your needs? When do you have time to deal with your emotional health? You don't.

It is my prayer that you will find unique healing in this book. There is a plethora of books on the market about how to raise godly children, be a better mom, and provide the best for your children. But this book focuses on *your* needs and the inner struggles *you* face. When you have won the battle over your own emotions, you will see the effects in your children. Wendy Stacy, former Oklahoma Single Mother of the Year, expressed it well: "When I was emotionally healed, my children followed suit."

In *The Single Mom and Her Rollercoaster Emotions*, you will discover eight destructive obstacles that stand in the way of successfully moving through the recovery process and experiencing renewed vitality as a single adult. The encumbering blockades of devastation, fear, anger and bitterness, anxiety, loneliness, low self-worth, guilt, and discouragement impede your journey. But there is good news. You don't have to live under their control. You can be the master of these roadblocks instead of them being the master over you. By making proactive choices, you will triumph by accepting "what is," trusting in God, exercising forgiveness, resting in the Father's peace, knowing your identity in Christ, abounding in God's grace, and expecting victory. God is moving you toward inner wholeness and full-powered joy.

CHAPTER ONE

From the Doom of Devastation to Accepting "What Is"

I would have despaired unless I had believed that I would see the goodness of the Lord in the land of the living. Wait for the Lord; be strong and let your heart take courage.
Psalm 27:13-14

Some moments stand as colossal monuments—moments in our lives that forever reside in our secret closets of remembrance. Days, months, and even years have no power to erase their shock and memory. I possess such a hiding place in my mind.

A crisp summer evening settled on my rooftop at 803 Glenn Drive, the kind of sundown that creates the mood to plant spring flowers the next morning. While I was envisioning my petunias and daffodils, my husband plopped himself down at the kitchen table. With a strange gaze and stuttering to find the words, he murmured under his breath, "I have something to tell you, and it's not going to be easy. This will hurt you." My first concern revolved around how this announcement would impact our toddlers, Jason and Sara.

His blank eyes and abnormal countenance toyed with my imagination. Leaning against the sink, I had a deafening sense that life as I knew it swayed on the brink of change. I didn't comprehend what was happening. I just knew that my enthusiasm for smelling gardenias vanished out the window. Maybe I would hear, "I lost my job, and we're moving." Or "I've been diagnosed with a serious illness." Whatever announcement loomed, I braced myself. *Ok, God. I can handle this.* I was wrong.

"Pam, I'm leaving."

"What do you mean, you're *leaving?*"

"I can't do this anymore. I can't live a lie any longer," he responded, his expression dismal. Had I entered outer space? Who was this alien? Frozen with shock, I watched him stand up, turn around, and exit the house. The garage door closed and he drove away, leaving our marriage in his rearview mirror.

I felt horror and denial. This was disloyalty at the cruelest level. How could this happen? In twelfth grade, he had captured my teenage heart with a stack of love letters that would sweep me into an eternal vow at twenty-three years old. What about the ten years of happy marital memories—happy for me, at least? I still loved this man. Jason and Sara displayed the best of both of us, carbon copies of the sweetest kind. Was I color blind? How did I miss the red flags indicating that he was miserable enough to begin another life under a separate roof? How could my husband's exit plans never once appear on my radar screen? In fact, a few days before, I had cuddled my three-year-old son as we giggled about love, assuring him that his family would stay together forever. In years past when I had heard such stories, I had wondered how the wife existed in such oblivion. Could she not see? I am an intuitive woman and read people well, but *this* announcement blindsided me to Venus and back. How do you recover from a betrayal that will forever alter the way you do life and family?

Millions of women around the planet encounter the same disturbing reality when a new season, or life cycle, emerges: single motherhood. You understand what such a role entails. Regardless of how you entered this season, the outcome remains the same for us all. We are left gathering the shattered pieces while our hearts labor on a *different* life journey of raising children alone.

My Rosy Satin Ribbon

I love God surprises. One afternoon after my husband left, God sent to my front porch a high-school friend I had not seen in years—Debbie Veale. Like a cherub on my doorstep with an envelope wrapped in a rosy ribbon, she blessed me with a gift: a money order for professional counseling. I knew I needed it, so I made my first visit. As I was leaving the appointment, the counselor's words sent me reeling: "Well, Pam, it's quite clear. You suffer from unresolved emotions."

What in the world are 'unresolved emotions'? I wondered. As a new single mom, I had no time to decode new phrases. The only vocabulary I understood came from a persistent two-year-old: "Mommy, gimme a gink of juice?" Or a three-year-old's question: "Mommy, why did Daddy move out?" Looking back, I understand what the counselor meant. Resembling a jam-packed ball of yarn, my entangled emotions refused to explain themselves, much less unravel so I could begin the healing process.

Friend, no one understands your plight and the albatross of responsibilities you carry more than other single moms do. Single motherhood remains *the* hardest job in this universe. Though it's wonderful having children, it's sometimes torturous, demoralizing, and filled with challenges that shatter your sense of survival, security, and purpose. Yoked to a never-ending cycle of seeming impossibilities, you resemble a passenger on a twisting rollercoaster, hurtling through loop-de-loops. Here's a resounding fact: *single motherhood is hard!*

Am I the Lone Ranger?

Webster's Dictionary defines the word *devastate* as *to lay waste.*[1] Amen to that! Devastation makes you feel as though you are the only one existing in the barren, foreign land called misfortune. There is no getting away from the pain. Everywhere you look, happy little married couples chat and hold hands, which only magnifies your inner voices that are saying:

- I am alone.
- I am defective.
- I am a victim, cheated out of *the good life*.

Whether you are never married, single again, or widowed or your husband is incarcerated, devastation hits us all the same. Our world has been turned upside down. Life as we knew it exists no more. The suffocation of what used to be feels like a slow death, where you are even losing contact with yourself. Although some women are content and glad to be single, all moms know the reality of having lost something dear to them: a mate, a dream, a comfortable financial situation, or a child through death or a custody battle.

What is the worst part? You can't fix it, and there's not even a shortcut for escaping this season of loss. Your desire to get beyond this tragedy clashes with the truth staring you square in the face: the only way *out of* the mess is to go *through it*. That is the nature of devastation. You want your circumstances better *now,* but the process demands *later.*

As cofounder of Arise Ministries, a national women's organization, I receive letters year round from single moms. I call this ten-inch stack of autobiographies my "What Do You Do?" stories. There is a common denominator among them: the feeling of ruin and a plea for help. Here are some examples.

Pam,

- *What do you do* when your husband dies, leaving you with a special-needs child?
- *What do you do* when your husband says, "I love my job. I love my children. I just don't love you?"
- *What do you do* when your husband announces he's having a baby with your closest cousin?
- *What do you do* when you are a pregnant newlywed and your husband is addicted to pornography?
- *What do you do* when your loneliness for a mate makes you shed tears on your pillow?

It's easy to feel as if you are the only one with a "What Do You Do?" story. You are not. Every single mom carries a life script containing some level of sorrow, discomfort, or frightening uncertainty.

Janie, a mom from Oklahoma City with two boys, shares her plight.

I was born in a very dysfunctional family. My parents divorced and hated each other. Mom dated men who were alcoholics, drug users, wife beaters, or child molesters. I was tossed to and fro through custody battles, not because my parents wanted me, but because they wanted to hurt each other more. When I was with my mother, we stayed in battered women's shelters. When I was with my father, I was abused by my stepmother. I ended up living in one foster home after another.

During my teenage years I was date-raped, leading to the discovery of my best friend—alcohol, which numbed my pain after hearing that my 4½ year old half-brother was literally beaten to death by one of my mother's boyfriends. So I thought I'd escape into marriage. Then after ten years, my husband demanded, "Choose either me or your God." That initiated my journey to single motherhood.

My life has not been easy, but God gave me Jesus. He's making my life count for His purpose, and He's given me a ministry encouraging women in prison. I do not regret the pain I've suffered; it's a strange kind of blessing that I've come to celebrate. My story is now His story, and His promise is now my promise: I can do all things through Christ who gives me strength.   —*Philippians 4:13*

Unbearable hardships fill Janie's testimony, but at the heart of it all lies her greatest gift: the power of choice. It was hers to choose whether to wallow in the cesspool of unfairness or grab hold of God's higher promise of divine opportunity.

My precious friend, you might be standing at the fork in the road of your recovery path. At what point will you bury your season of desolation? When will you change the compass of your thoughts and trust God for His? Are you ready to announce to your soul that you have grieved long enough, and it is time to move forward? You cannot reverse the past, but you can determine the duration of the despair it causes.

Devastation happens when life doesn't turn out the way we planned. Every hero in the Bible trailed through the temporary desert of adversity without understanding why *this* happened to *him or her*. Alone, confused, and exhausted to the point of death, many questioned why they were in these situations. Don't you think that is the hardest part, adjusting to "what is" when you want "what was" or "what will be"?

Moses contended with the Israelites' hunger in the wilderness: *"Lord, why are you doing this to me? This job is too much. How can I take care of these people by myself? Just kill me and end my miserable life."*[2] *In spite of this,* Moses emerged as the most celebrated prophet in Judaism.

Elijah ran from Ahab and Jezebel and begged to God, *"I have had enough. Just let me die. I alone am left in this fight."*[3] In spite of this, Elijah found God's favor and was taken up to Heaven in a chariot of fire.

Job cursed God: *"Why didn't I die at birth? I wish I had been born dead and then buried, never to see the light of day."*[4] In spite of this, Job gained the reputation of a man who lived righteously.

What will your *in spite of this* look like? How will you allow God to strengthen and empower you on your journey? Your *in spite of this* catapults you into a renewed relationship with Christ, showcasing God's goodness in a way that astounds and blesses not just you but everyone God brings into your path. Rest assured— God never wastes devastation.

The Book of Psalms resonates with episodes of King David dangling from the cliff of destruction. However, his obedience to God formed the basis of his prayers for deliverance. I love the raw emotions of David's helplessness: *"I would have despaired unless I believed I would see the goodness of the Lord in the land of the living."*

Did you notice? David *would have* despaired, but he didn't. He *would have* toppled over, but he didn't. He *would have* lost heart, but he didn't. Why?

- David lived with faith in a power greater than himself.
- David used his hardships as a platform for God's unyielding faithfulness.
- David employed God as his keeper, consoler, and liberator.
- David believed in God's character over his own circumstances.

King David believed and professed God's goodness. What happened as a result? God rushed to David's defense as a mom rushes to pull her toddler out of the street. When you are desperate and you turn to God, He shows up. The same God who took up residence in David's despair takes up space in yours.

When you are desperate and you turn to God, He shows up.

The first component of overcoming adversity is understanding the nature and purpose of devastation. However, like getting a hot-air balloon to lift off the ground, a second component is required.

ACCEPTING "WHAT IS"

My times are in Your hand.
Psalm 31:15

Two weeks after I officially received my new title, *single mother,* I slouched on the curb, dejected and sobbing. People driving by could gawk at this woman in despair. Carol, my well-meaning neighbor, saw me through her window and felt the need to console me. Arm in arm we sat. She listened. Married a second time, she understood the trauma of starting life over again. I remember her counsel. It stung, making me furious. It didn't feed my hope of returning to normalcy any time soon.

"Pam, you're going to have to accept this."

"Accept it? Are you kidding? Why should I acquiesce to a newfound lifestyle I didn't ask for?"

She counseled, "You have no choice. It's a must for your survival."

Follow the Yellow Brick Road

The stage you are in as a single mom determines your ability to stomach this word: *acceptance.* If you are like me, at first it made you boil, boil, *boil.* Perhaps one of these questions fits your situation:

- Why should I accept this divorce (or my husband's death or my children's verbal abuse)?
- Why should I tolerate the unfairness that I am getting no child support?
- Why should I have this baby when the father loves another woman?
- Why should I exercise forgiveness when the judge awarded custody to my children's father?
- Why should I let God have His way when He has let me down?

In *The Wizard of Oz,* the yellow brick road led Dorothy and her friends to their solution. God is leading you on the same trail. Three golden bricks lie before you, pointing you to God's destination of wholesome purpose and Christ-centered joy. You travel the journey one brick at a time.

Brick #1—The Crisis Stage

This stage leaves you in a state of numbed disbelief called denial. You cry out, "This can't be happening to me." Although it is a natural, physiological mechanism protecting you from the enormity of the trauma, it still hurts. For months you may even deny the reality of the loss in order to avoid the intensity of the shock. The grief that follows is real because life now as a single mother is scary. You are vulnerable and lack energy.

After my husband left, a furnace of disbelief burned beneath the surface, stoking my unsettledness and never-ending questions. Somehow, the sensible "old Pam" vanished, and the absentminded "new Pam" moved in. I found myself stashing potholders in the oven, placing my car keys in the soap dish, and sleeping at the foot of my bed. I had no strategy for coping with my upside-down world. Everything felt skewed through a lens of impaired memory and blurry thoughts. I recall one night sitting straight up in bed with a scream of anger that carried all the way to Sara's room, waking her up. My parenting attentiveness diminished, too. My sister Vicki, who lived thirty minutes away, left grooves in the highway from all her visits in an effort to keep me afloat. I honestly didn't know how I had gotten myself into this mess.

Beloved friend, if you are in the crisis stage, don't despair for long. The complexities of life rotate in seasons. This stage will pass (did I hear you rejoice?). However, in the meantime, don't give your emotions too much authority or allow them to define what is true. Rather, trust Jesus to lead you out. Find new ways to depend on Christ by believing in His faithfulness, even though you don't *feel* like it. What you *feel* does not define what is true, and it is a poor guide in this stage. Emotions are nothing more than a rollercoaster, wild and unpredictable. Hang on tight, and above all, don't let go or give up.

Brick #2—The Transition Stage

Though you will jump back and forth from brick to brick, you will eventually ease out of the crisis stage into a period of reflection, accompanied by an aching sense of sadness and loneliness and a keen awareness of the magnitude of your loss. Others will try to make you feel better: *"Come on. It's time to put this behind you and move forward."* I recall my best friend giving me that advice and it didn't help one bit. Like a screeching cat with paws held upright, my inner self flared back. My thoughts went something like this:

- *I can't move on. I'm empty and disconnected.*
- *I don't know myself anymore.*
- *I have lost interest in activities.*
- *I need to "fly the coop" to a Hawaiian island and never come back.*

However, deep down I knew I could not escape. Neither can you. Why is that? You are the "single—solo—solitary" mother. How could you leave? Who would take little Mary to piano lessons or monitor your teenager's curfew? Honolulu is out of the question.

The transition stage defines itself well: it is a time of developing a balance between the old and the new while seeking avenues of proper healing. I found an organized support group on grief. It served as a wonderful safety net during my reconstruction. I began discovering innovative ways of letting Jesus rule my thoughts and tame my emotions, not to mention my glorious return to *mothering well*.

However, right when you think you are making great headway in this stage, something unanticipated flares up. I remember driving down the road whistling a happy tune when the sheer sight of a man holding a woman's hand gave my heart a whack and—*bam*—within seconds, I found myself hunkered in the dugout of sadness. Don't worry. That is the nature of the transition stage. It won't last forever.

Brick #3—The Emergence Stage

Aren't you glad that this third phase is built on God's agenda for recovery? After a laborious journey, you are emerging as a healthy, single woman. While it doesn't mean you always feel happy or will ever return to the *old you*, it does mean God is fashioning a *new you*, an exquisite woman of value created to flourish in your singleness and in your relationship with Jesus Christ.

This stage brought me such joy. Blinders lifted and my anger at the unfairness evolved into hope. I felt as though I were standing on a high-rise, observing the horizon. The exhilarating prospects of how God could use every particle of my past pain for His higher calling set my heart aflame. I couldn't wait to find out the answers to these questions:

- What could God do with a single mom who, from the inside out, yielded herself to Him?
- How could Jesus convert dark shades of disappointment into colorful hues of possibility?
- Did Jesus have *my* "What Do You Do?" story in mind when He promised to give life abundantly?
- Is it true that some things fall apart so that better things can fall together?

Through God's telescope, I saw my trauma burst into thousands of brilliant stars, in expectation of His plan for me to use my divorce to speak of His renown. Friend, remember the petunias and daffodils I never planted? Spring had "sprung," and the magnolias and lilies that grew instead smelled divine.

Some things fall apart so that better things can fall together.

What Is God's Job? What Is Yours?

I love the Serenity Prayer. Its teaching on acceptance and redefining roles relieves our belief that it is up to us to fix the broken pieces.

God, grant me the serenity to accept the things I cannot change, the courage to change the things I can, and the wisdom to know the difference.

One single mom expressed the theme well.

No matter how hard I try, cry, pray or stray, some realities in my life and home I have no power to change. Understanding what this looks like helps me just be, not do or even say. By relaxing my grip of control, doing what I can, and trusting God with the results, I'm learning to accept my temporary chaos.

When we heal our emotions God's way, we break away from the feeling of entrapment. Whose job is it to change hearts? Whose job is it to let God be God? Notice three principles concerning our role and God's role.

Identification

Our job encompasses identifying what cannot be repaired. Moms are menders at heart. We want our family ducks in a row, but when relationships break, certain fragments cannot be glued together. They are called "unfixables." I had my list. How about you? Are any of these in your catalogue?

- I can't make my husband love me.
- I can't bring my deceased husband back to life.
- I can't coerce my boyfriend into marrying me now that I'm pregnant.
- I can't manipulate my children to choose me over their dad.
- I can't talk to my son about his father because he is adopted.
- I can't rescind the conviction that landed my husband in jail.
- I can't force my child to accept responsibility as a parent, even though I'm now a single mom.

Give yourself the three-question test.

- Can I fix it?
- Can I change it?
- Can I reverse it?

If not, let go. Refuse to let it get under your skin. If you can't control the problem, it has no right to control you. Acknowledge what's unchangeable (for now, anyway), remembering that just because it is outside your ability to control it doesn't mean the Lord is not at work. In the meantime, accept "what is," and trust God with "what isn't." God works mightily in us through His Spirit to advance us toward His highest and best.

As a single mom, you are like a woman in a circus trapeze act. The bar represents your security, the way you have learned to deal with all life's difficulties and sorrows. But God has tossed you another trapeze bar, one that promises to swing you in the direction of a purpose and joy you never dreamed possible. The question becomes, "Will you relinquish the bar of familiarity for the handle of the unknown?" Though it is not familiar to you, it is familiar to God, already written before the foundations of the earth in His manual for you. You are freefalling into the wondrous experience of how God will remain strong in you. Can you let go of worrying and calculating with one hand and take hold of God's promise for divine healing with the other?

I recall the afternoon when God barged into my trapeze act and beckoned me to trust Him with a new direction in life. My husband and I had been separated for two years, and I was growing weary while I waited. While browsing in a craft store, I mused, *Will this ever end?* An arrow from God Himself pierced my heart, stopping my cart dead in its tracks. *"Pam, your husband is not coming back. It's o-v-e-r. O-v-e-r!"* I was stunned but somewhat relieved. It sank in. Something snapped, and I threw up my arms. Running through the store, swishing past surprised shoppers, I cheered out loud, *"I'm free. I'm free."* My devastation bled into acceptance, opening the wondrous view of my new life from the helicopter of God's perspective.

Friend, maybe you need God's strength to let go and accept your devastation. Perhaps it's time to give your preconceived idea of marriage and family a proper burial. You didn't get what you most wanted. It died, but God is not finished with your story.

Isaiah 43 encourages:

Do not call to mind the former things, or ponder things of the past.

Behold, I will do something new. Now it will spring forth. Will you not be aware of it? I will even make a roadway in the wilderness, rivers in the desert.

What is keeping you from complying with God's "what is" and trusting Him with your "what ifs"? Are you ready for the surprise package of His "something new"?

Activation

This remains our job, as well. Though we might not be able to repair the marriage, alter what others think, afford a nanny, or exhibit "happy" thoughts about our children's stepmother, we can change some things. By seeking a healthier perspective, increasing our reliance on God, turning away from sin, avoiding ungodly words, and letting go of our false belief that our circumstances are greater than God's ability to intercede, we can redirect our thinking. When we play spiritual dominoes and trust God by standing up our disappointments back to back, God collapses every obstacle that blocks our progress.

My hardest domino to knock down revolved around my Barbie Dream House persona. You recall Barbie's perfect world: an eighteen-inch waist (for real?), Mr. Charming for a hubby, a life of high heels and faultless children who never rebelled. Certainly she never found herself in divorce court. That was my fairytale. I wanted it all back: my Ken, my original family unit, my house with the white picket fence.

Fixating on what we don't have hinders the greater blessings we could have if we chose acceptance over reluctance. A bold-hearted friend mustered up enough courage to scold me one afternoon. "Pam, quit seeing yourself as a victim; get out of the quicksand of self-pity. Take advantage of the possibilities before you. Start behaving like God's doing a miracle in you, because He is." Truth sometimes stings.

Fixating on what we don't have hinders the greater blessings we could have if we chose acceptance over reluctance.

Multiplication

This job belongs to God. The last phrase of the Serenity Prayer speaks of the wisdom in distinguishing what you can't change from what you can. The result brings you a storehouse of God's blessings: His nearness, His comfort, His joy, His security. It's a win-win for all. There is no formula to follow for receiving spiritual strength. It involves choosing to step into God's broader plan of transforming you into the empowered single mom you never knew you could be.

Friend, why does it feel safer to keep yourself in a box when, in reality, you have no control at all? What's keeping you from releasing your negative emotions and trusting Christ with radical courage? Why not receive the invitation to watch the Almighty revolutionize your "What Do You Do?" story? Turn from the visible impossibilities to the invisible opportunities by meditating on the comforting power of Jesus' words.

In John 10:10, Christ proclaimed, *"I have come that you might have life, and have it* abundantly." What does *abundantly* look like in your scenario? Its Greek root word means "superfluously; life to its fullest."[5] Jesus gives all that sustains life. Are you ready for this kind of a God surplus?

The Mother of the Year Award

A mom like you celebrated her child. She embraced the tasks of nursing, burping, and changing her baby's diapers. Giggling at her son's antics, she enjoyed watching him play with his sibling. She kissed his boo-boos and cuddled him when he cried.

She, too, faced devastation one day. Her child was summoned not to a court battle but to the cross. Mary, the mother of Jesus Christ, understands your challenge of accepting circumstances you never wanted.

You ask, *God, how can I do this alone? I'm only one. I'm "Mommy" not "Mommy and Daddy." This situation breaks my heart. My children didn't ask for this. It's not their fault Daddy doesn't live here. I hate this, God! And by the way, while You're listening, let me ask You one more question. Are my kids going to turn out ok?*

We sometimes lose sight that God loves single moms. I've often wondered why Joseph, Jesus' earthly father, was never mentioned in the Bible after chapter 2 of Luke. Could it be that Mary found herself made single again by her husband's death? We don't know. If that's the case, we understand why God is passionate about a widow's plight.

Whether Mary emerged single or married doesn't matter. God doesn't check our marital status before our name appears on His *Favored List*. He grants His mercy for one reason alone: His love. Why? Is it because of something we have done? No, God adores us because He chooses to do so, not because of our merit or résumé of good deeds. We don't understand radical intimacy like that, but God is enamored with your loveliness and longs to enter into a deep friendship, crowning you with radiant splendor and honor.

God doesn't check our marital status before our name appears on His *Favored List*.

Friend, *God loves you!* You don't need to be perfect to possess Jesus' favor. In the Bible, did Christ heal the hurting because of anything they had done? Was He looking for people who had it all together, or was He longing for those who would love Him in return? He comes to you in the same manner, knocking at the door of your "what is." Will you answer?

The Supreme Invite

Beloved single mom, maybe you have never heard this good news about Christ's unconditional love. Perhaps you have never known Jesus, but you desire His compassion, comfort, and grace. This moment stands as His appointed time for you to surrender your single motherhood to Him. He is waiting. Why not turn it over to Him?

Dear Lord, I turn away from the kind of life I have been living. I ask forgiveness for being the master controller of my life. I choose Your way by coming to the end of my own resources. I give myself to You. In Jesus' name, amen.

Sister, if you yielded your life to Jesus, I'm sending a shout-out of congratulation. Something magnificent just happened! You entreated the Spirit of the living God to invest His power and presence in you, ensuring an eternal destiny with Him. Hallelujah!

God is on the move. Let the curtain of His wonders and profuse goodness arise on your new heart. Opportunity awaits you.

Whispers from Jesus

You think you will never recover. You will. I knew the day you gave birth that this season would arrive. Let Me refresh you with My company. You have journeyed through loss. You can't accept things right now, but you can accept My invitation to carry you one day at a time. I am bringing beauty out of the ashes of your burnt dreams. When you feel devastated, hear My whisper, "I cherish you, My love."

Silent Reflection

1. Describe your "What Do You Do?" story.
2. Which of the three stages represents your position?
3. Define your "unfixables."
4. Do you see devastation or opportunity? Explain your thoughts.
5. What is the recurring theme in Psalm 42?

Gentle Respite for the Soul

God Helps

Psalm 18:6—*In my distress, I called upon the Lord and cried to my God for help. He heard my voice out of His temple, and my cry for help came into His ears.*

Psalm 28:7—*The Lord is my strength and shield; my heart trusts in Him, and I am helped. Therefore my heart exults, and with my song I shall thank Him.*

God Reigns

Romans 8:28—*And we know that God works everything together for good to those who love God and are called according to His purposes.*

Psalm 103:19—*God has established His throne in the heavens and His sovereignty rules over all.*

God Turns Devastation into Delight

Jeremiah 31:13b—*I will comfort them turning their sorrows into joy. I will bless My people.*

Psalm 30:5—*His favor is for a lifetime. Weeping may last for the night, but a shout of joy comes in the morning.*

CHAPTER TWO

From Fear of the Unknown to Trusting in God

*I sought the Lord, and He heard me, and
delivered me from all my fears.*
Psalms 34:4

Her name was Hagar. Genesis chronicles her life as a mother whose desperate plight tugs at every woman's heartstrings. She was an Egyptian maidservant, a foreigner far from her native land who served as a slave in the tent of Sarah and Abraham. Sarah was barren, so she gave this handmaiden to her husband as his concubine, and Ishmael was born. Fourteen years later, Sarah bore a child, Isaac.

That's not the end of this "happy" little story. It's one of the most toxic family dramas in the Bible. Sarah and Hagar despised one another, and Hagar found herself kicked out of the household with a teenage son. The Bible reports, "So Abraham rose early in the morning and took bread and a skin of water and gave them to Hagar and the boy and sent them away. And she departed and wandered about in the wilderness of Beersheba."

Hagar, a refugee stripped of familiar surroundings, rejected and mistreated by those in her camp, lay susceptible to desert bandit thieves and wild boars. However, above all the horrors of the unexpected hazards ahead, she remained first and foremost a s-i-n-g-l-e mother, frantic over the well-being of her child. Does this sound familiar?

Fear of the unknown is the nature of being a single mother. *What dangers await me? How can I do this alone? Will it* always *be like this?* I'm sure Hagar was much like you. She dreamed as a young girl of the autumn day when she could nurture her children under the roof of an adoring companion, a leader to provide for her nest, a strong man to serve as the backbone of steel in her children's sense of security. But now, every smidgen of that dream remained only a painful token of a shattered fantasy.

Invisible Sharks

I've never met a single mom who did not struggle at some point with fear of the unknown. A woman cannot thrive under the duress of being everything for everybody. It is easy for life to become an onslaught of twenty-foot waves, rising up and nearly thwarting every stroke to survive. Physical challenges are difficult enough, but the emotional whitecaps that break over the top feel like the final blow in holding you under.

I know the horror of standing on both feet and facing the approaching tsunami with a toddler in each arm. Every single mom has battled with fears that ripple right below the water's surface, those invisible sharks of insecurity, inferiority, and seeming impossibility. Read the real-life testimonies I have received over the years. No wonder you teeter totter between trusting in God and hitting the ocean floor.

Insecurities
- One minute my former husband wants to be a family, and the next minute he doesn't. How long will this go on?
- I feel nervous when my son is on the Internet. That's why his dad left—pornography. What if my son gets hooked, too?

Inferiorities
- I was forced out of my apartment. I'm now living with my parents. How long will this humiliating arrangement last?
- I have four kids, and I'm fifty-eight pounds overweight. What man would ever look at me? The mirror tells it all.

Impossibilities
- I cry myself to sleep every night with my silent companion: loneliness. It's a dark shadow that never leaves me.
- I'm a college student, but I'm failing two classes. I don't have time to study. What if I can't get my degree?

My friend, what's your deepest insecurity, inferiority, or seeming impossibility? These frightening thoughts scurry in your mind like cockroaches in the dark: *What if things get worse?* or *What if things stay the same?* Layer upon layer they build strongholds, from blind panic attacks concerning your todays to sleepless nights regarding your tomorrows. The present wouldn't be scary if you knew that the future would be different.

The Ferris Wheel or the Screaming Mimi?

Handling fear properly is one of the toughest problems we will ever face, and our success depends on the approach we take. How are you harnessing your greatest fears? Which carnival ride have you chosen? The Ferris wheel, the one that goes round and round until it stops, leaving you to view what's below from God's perspective, or the Screaming Mimi, the rollercoaster that clickety-clacks along its track, trapping you behind its deceptive safety bars?

The Bible declares that two "rides" or vehicles order our thoughts. God's thoughts are propelled by divine authority, safety, and protection. Satan's thoughts are driven by intimidation, condemnation, and defeat. God's primary focus is love. Satan's primary focus is fear—fear of the unknown, of others, of failure, of shame, of being alone. When we live in terror, we have chosen to fall under the influence of the rollercoaster's fright. And what kind of ride is that? It's one that keeps us unsettled, creating spiritual amnesia by causing us to forget what God has done in the past. Its carriage zooms around every crest and curve, refusing to stop and let us catch our breaths.

Good grief, friend. Do something about it. Grab your purse and get off that rollercoaster! *But how?* you ask.

Fear creates spiritual amnesia by causing us to forget what God has done in the past.

The Warrior Within

When you received Christ as your Savior, God placed in you

through the power of the Holy Spirit His strength, wisdom, and hope. You did not receive a permanent nature of faintheartedness and helplessness but one of intestinal fortitude, godly might, and best of all an anchored mind that could pray down God's "calm" no matter what the circumstances. Through God's Spirit, you can take the edge off doom and gloom and replace it with settled peace. There's a God-implanted "new you" inside, a person capable of hushing into silence your most frightful forebodings.

I know what you're thinking. *Living under my dark cloud has become a part of my lifestyle, my personality. I eat with it, parent with it, fold clothes with it. How do I break through this distressing barricade into that oasis of relief?* Friend, do what the disciples did one night when they found themselves drowning in their fears. They shouted, "Lord, save me." Something happens when the presence of Jesus Christ invades our darkness.

Lessons in the Deep

It was one the most awe-inspiring nights in the disciples' lives. They had witnessed Jesus feeding 5,000 men with only five loaves and two fish. (Including women and children, it was likely 25,000 people!) The multitudes gasped in astonishment, for the reality had finally landed in every doubtful mind that the Son of God's feet were currently treading upon planet earth. The Scriptures point out that immediately after the massive fish banquet, Jesus instructed the disciples to get into their boat and flee to the other side of the lake. He had another miracle in mind.

While they rowed in the wee hours of the night, a vicious rainstorm came up and pushed the disciples farther and farther from shore. They were already exasperated, confused, and disillusioned that Jesus had sent them in the boat in the first place, knowing full well that the storm was coming. After all, He was God. Couldn't He have spared them the trauma? They battled the storm for almost nine hours. Where was He? Then, Jesus came to them, walking on the water. Hallelujah!

They should have been rejoicing. They should have remembered that Jesus was their stronghold in times of trouble. They should have remembered David's words that no matter where they go, God's right hand would hold them fast. They should have remembered God's promise to Moses out of the burning bush that He sees their afflictions. They should have remembered the lesson of Abraham that God always provides. They should have. They should have . . . but they didn't. Fear of the unknown had overpowered all they knew about the character of God and all the lessons that Jesus had taught them, and all they could think about were their fears.[1]

Yet Jesus came to them in His perfect timing through the gales that threatened to destroy them.

And when the disciples saw Him walking on the sea, they were frightened, saying, "It is a ghost." And they cried out for fear. But immediately Jesus spoke to them saying, "Take courage, it is I, do not be afraid."   —Matthew 14:26-27

Then Jesus extended the once-in-a-lifetime chance for Peter to enter the upper floor of Heaven's domain, the opportunity to literally walk above the boisterous waters and triumph over his circumstances. Jesus offered, "Come." And Peter did. He rose by faith over the elements of nature, but as soon as he took his focus off Jesus and considered the blustery waves below, he began to sink into the dreadful "what ifs": *What if I drown? What if there's no one to take over my business? What if my wife struggles to survive without me? What if my brother Andrew becomes destitute?*

Then Peter voiced the three words that summoned Jesus to the lake in the first place. Those three words represented the very reason that Jesus came to the earth. Those three words had the clout to shut the mouth of Satan and open wide the gates to Heaven's utmost treasures. Today, they are what you and I need every time we find ourselves trapped on the rollercoaster of fear. Peter screamed forth, *"Lord, save me!"*

Jesus allowed the disciples to reach the extremity of their need. He knew of the coming weather long before it tattered their boat to pieces. He understood the nature of the disciples to initially cling to fear over faith, and He recognized that their trust in Him was still in its infancy. Yet Jesus was bringing them to a place of brokenness and then stripping them of their skepticism that Christ alone would deliver them from their gravest threats. The Messiah, the Ruler of the Waters, was teaching Peter that focusing on Him in times of frightful danger yielded even greater power than the turbulent waters below. Peter had witnessed the futility of cowering from the thunder and the menace of the waves. Ultimately, he would enter the history of Christendom simply because he spoke three itty-bitty words, "Lord, save me."

What if you said, "Lord, save me!" What happens in the spiritual realm when you bring Jesus to the forefront of your consciousness? What could that phrase accomplish in your personal life? How could bringing God's presence into your situation boost your ability to cope? Friend, it takes courage to say, "Lord, save me!" with a heart ready to make the necessary changes.

Can you say that now: *Lord, save me!* Yes, Lord . . .

- Save me from thinking I need another man to take care of my family when You are my husband.
- Save me from believing what is visible more than I believe what is invisible.
- Save me from seeing my family as broken when You are the head of this household.
- Save me from hindering my children's faith because mine falters.
- Save me from insulting You by yielding to my fears when You are right here.
- Save me from beating myself up when my child doesn't make wise choices.

I am best friends with that last one, and it is a nightmare. I taught my son, Jason, godly principles. I read bedtime Bible stories emphasizing the greatness of God. We sang fun songs in the car about the love of Jesus. He attended Christian camps in the summer. I modeled Christ. But in ninth grade, he chose a different route: drugs. As a mom, I comprehend the horror of feeling like a failure. I understand what it means to sleep on the floor beside the front door waiting for your child to get home by his curfew. I've experienced the repulsion of having the high school call because the drug dogs located his car. I remember my sickness of heart when I rounded the corner of the house and discovered a ladder propped outside his upstairs window for a secret, middle-of-the-night escapade. At the time, I was teaching a Bible class of over 250 women! Where did I go wrong? I called out multiple times, *"Save me, Lord. Save me! Save him, Lord. Save him."* What happens when we cry out for the Lord? Matthew 12:28-31 states, *"And immediately Jesus stretched out His hand and took hold of him."*

During this season with my son, I learned I had only one of two choices: die in the swamp of worry and helplessness or radically trust in God and His power to save the one I loved. Friend, today Jason is a wonderful husband and father of two children who loves Jesus with all his heart, soul, mind, and body. I'm passionate in telling moms raising spiritually rebellious children to never give up. Never stop believing and never stop praying. In James 5:16, God's Word promises that *the prayers of the righteous availeth much.*

Friend, Jesus' hand in the storm is not just any hand. It is the divine bridge between your angst and His answers, your havoc and His hope, your destruction and His direction. It is continually extended for all who transfer their grip of self over to Him. What is keeping your hand from reaching up to Jesus?

Courage Is Fear Holding on One Minute Longer

Dear single mom, you can do it. Don't give up! *Yes, single motherhood is hard,* but God stands strong in you. Your nature is to easily fear, but God's nature is to continually save. Do you believe that?

Webster's defines courage as a quality of mind that enables one to encounter difficulties and danger with firmness.[2] I like that. From where does that steadfastness come? It arises from rock-solid belief in the Almighty's determination to rescue, no matter what seems impossible to you. Over four hundred times in the Bible, God addresses our tendencies to fear. Throughout the ages, God has consoled His people: "I see the situation. Do not be afraid."

- To Moses the Lord encouraged, "Do not be afraid, for I have handed your enemy over to you with his whole army and land."

- To Joshua the Lord reassured, "Do not be afraid, for I have given them into your hand and not one of them will be able to withstand you."
- To Abraham the Lord said, "Do not be afraid, for I am your shield, your very great reward."
- To Paul the Lord instructed, "Do not be afraid. Keep on speaking and do not be silent."
- To Jarius Jesus said, "Do not be afraid. Just believe and she will be healed."

Perhaps your greatest crisis of faith revolves around whether God will save you, too. God beckons, "Beloved, single mother, do not be afraid. For I know the way I am taking you. I will not let you down. Take Me at My Word. Believe."

So, will you? The antidote to fear of the unknown is knowing that God will overcome its grip. Courage evens out your emotional rollercoaster. However, unless you implement this next act of faith, your courage has no power source.

TRUSTING IN GOD

I will trust, and will not be afraid; for the Lord God is my strength and my song, and He has become my salvation.
Isaiah 12:2

A rock climber found himself dangling for dear life against a mountain crag. The expansion bolt he had set in the rock had broken loose, causing him to flop against the cliff face. He lifted his head in desperation and cried out, "Help! Is there anyone up there?" But there was no answer. He bellowed again, "Help! Is there anyone up there?" There was still no response. One last time he pleaded, "Help! Is there anyone up there?" Finally a reply came back, "Yes, it is I, God. Turn loose." The mountaineer pondered a moment and answered in return, "Is there anyone else up there?"

Before you chuckle, you might consider that we resemble the climber. That is the way we often view God. He is a stupendous Creator, having thrust His paintbrush of brilliant colors across the early dawn; however, when "push comes to shove," we might not want to accept the type of help He is offering us. How shortsighted of us! Perhaps we've forgotten what would have happened had the sportsman let go of the rope. Don't you think God would have caught him on the way down and lifted him to new heights, revealing glorious sights he could never have seen otherwise?

In Good Hands

To *speak* about trusting the Lord and actually *doing* it remain two different things. It is easy to rely on God when you have some measure of control in the situation (or at least you think you do), but when it's totally beyond your ability to fix, trusting God seems like a daunting risk. Deep down inside, you don't want God to let you down. *What if I trusted God and He didn't come through? Where would I turn then?*

I know what it feels like to place your confidence in God and not receive the answer for which you had hoped. I was separated for two years, and not a day went by that I didn't believe God would restore my marriage. But He didn't. Wouldn't it have been easier for me to have gone my own way those years instead of wasting my optimism and becoming emotionally shattered the day it was officially over? It was that "done moment" that provoked this brutal question: *Pam, do you* really *trust God?* I'm not so sure I did, to be honest. Yet God's goodness lifted me up like a wounded sparrow and He whispered, "Trust Me, Pam. Trust Me." It was a scary moment. Fear of the unknown, of letting go, and of trusting God can sometimes feel ten times worse than the current pain. But when the Holy Spirit's comfort and strength collide with your loss, you are in good hands.

The Trust Factor

Relying on God requires placing your confidence in another, transferring ownership of something precious to you to a caretaker. When you trust God with your greatest fears, you have chosen to release the outcome into the hands of someone who can handle it better than you can. God challenges us to consider the source of our faith: *Do I trust God or myself?*

Consider the source of your faith. *Do I trust God or myself?*

Trusting also encompasses the idea of sacrifice—giving away

something of value. It costs you something. Your cost might involve giving up control or refusing to worry. Whatever it is, you have put to death something close to you. When you abandon yourself to a loving God, the assurance of His faithfulness gives way to hope. You can then lay your fears down on God's altar as an act of obedience, much as Abraham did with his son Isaac.

Friend, what fear needs to be assigned to God's care? Your responses to the test of trusting determine the extent of your victories. The deeper the fear surrendered to Him, the greater His blessings and the strengthening of your faith. Big fears equal big miracles. Little fears equal little miracles. The bottom line is that freedom from fear lies on the other side of trusting.

The Bigness of God—So What?

Has anyone ever told you, "Well, you just need to trust God"? It's kind of irritating, if you want to know the truth. As much as you stand in awe that God made the Milky Way plus another 100 billion galaxies, this truth doesn't answer how you are going to qualify for health insurance or how you are going to manage your migraine-inducing panic attacks. How can you funnel the "Milky Way God" down into your fears, so you have a tangible piece of His power, something sufficient for breaking the visible strongholds of your nagging uncertainties?

Your deep-rooted trust in God remains only as effective as the extent to which you rely on His character. Do you know the qualities of God that grant courage? Can you pinpoint how His distinctiveness makes a difference in your fears? Do you call on the attributes of God that empower you to overcome? Knowing who God is and what He does fuels your trust factor.

Peekaboo—I "Seek" You

Sometimes we think finding God is like a game of hide and seek. We search for Him under every hedge, as if He is hunkered down ten feet below the dirt. In fact, the Lord is not hiding from us. In Jeremiah 29:13, He exults, "When you seek me, *you will find me*, when you search for me wholeheartedly." Friend, God wants to be found. He is out in the wide-open, waving a red flag. *Here I am, over here. I'm seeking you, too.*

I love it. God reveals in Scripture that He sees the plight of the single mother. Remember Hagar, the first single mother in the Bible? I'm sure Sarah and Hagar had found themselves engaged in yet another squabble when Hagar fled to the stream to count to ten. As she sat there pregnant and feeling misunderstood, an angel of the Lord noticed her distress, and the Lord spoke through the angel.

Hagar, what are you doing? Where are you going? Return to your mistress and I will greatly multiply your descendants and they will be many. You will bear a son, Ishmael. Yes, I have seen your affliction.

Imagine sitting by that stream, feeling exasperated and abandoned. What would you have done if an angel appeared with a message from God? Here is the good part about the encounter: it wasn't just any ol' message. It contained a detailed promise. God Almighty saw Hagar. He called her by name. He knew her occupation, her trouble, her child's name in the womb, and her destiny. Friend, God knew. God saw. God made a proclamation at the stream that day for all future single mothers to remember: *I am a God that sees.* He sees your plight in living color.

- God sees your health issues that began April 2.
- God sees your bank account that will be overdrawn at 3:15 p.m. tomorrow.
- God sees your prostitution with the three men who paid your March rent.
- God sees your son's trouble with the bully wearing the red cap.

God sees what rattles your sense of security. He has promised to bring His unchangeable character and unconditional love into your darkness because God remains . . .

- Sovereign—God rules over all, in accordance with His holy nature.
- Omniscient—God possesses all knowledge.

- Omnipotent—God retains all power.
- Just—God does what is right.

Likewise, in your single-mother world . . .

- God *always* remains in control. *Fear not. I've got it covered.*
- God *always* knows the future. *Fear not. I will be there when you get there.*
- God *always* possesses unlimited power. *Fear not. If your "what if" becomes your "what is," I can handle it.*
- God *always* performs what is right. *Fear not. Nobody can mistreat you and ultimately get away with it if you have faith in Me.*

If your "what if" becomes your "what is," God can handle it.

Wanda Pratt, single mother of NBA superstar Kevin Durant of the Oklahoma City Thunder, testifies:

After becoming an empty nester and a divorcee I struggled with fear of the unknown—"my" unknown; but what God showed me is that my unknown was not "His" unknown. Because I am the righteousness of God in Jesus Christ, I am completely safe as I keep my eyes stayed on Him and not me. That may sound like religious jargon, but it's a true fact and a choice every single mother must make. When you look into the future and choose to see Jesus and not yourself, your thoughts become as bright as the morning sun.

You can trust God with fears of the unknown. Why? *Because God sees.*

More Than the Crows

It was likely a spring afternoon in the hilly terrain of Lower Galilee when Jesus shared passionate life lessons with His new disciples. Jesus understood their tendency to miss the joys of today and live in the fears of tomorrow. But I believe that Jesus saw other faces in the gathering of students that day—yours and mine—and He instructed:

Beloved disciples, do not be anxious for your life concerning what you will eat, drink, or wear. Look at those crows. They are incapable of holding jobs or planting crops or gathering the harvest into barns, but My Father sustains them. Don't you think you are more valuable than they? If My Father takes care of them, how much more will He take care of you, a creation made in His image? So stop being fearful. Quit thrusting yourself into tomorrow's possibilities. When you put My Father first, He will provide. Live only within the boundaries of today. Do not think of future "what ifs." It is senseless to add tomorrow's cares to those of today.[3]

What was Jesus saying? He put forth two truths. First, allowing ourselves to live in fear of the unknown is a crippling act of disobedience. Living with a spirit of fear comes when a heart lacks the genuine belief that God is good enough, big enough, and faithful enough to attend to our needs. Second, dwelling on our fears robs us of the chance to see God's hand of mercy in our present. Bringing tomorrow's worries into today's grace blinds us to God's wonders.

Friend, God will provide. What is it you need today? It is impossible for Jesus to abandon His followers. I have never seen a single mom who placed her trust in Christ and was left in an isolated ditch. God takes care of His own. It is the essence of His nature, and He can never act in a way that contradicts or defames His character.

I met Stevi, a single mother from Kentucky, at a conference. She waited for me afterward for some counsel. I noticed her from afar, a woman with a walking cane, silky, autumn-colored hair, and a set of teeth that likely appeared on the front cover of *Vogue* the previous month. I strained to hear her words as the presence of Jesus fell on our conversation.

I came to Christ when I was in third grade. I graduated with a degree as a dental hygienist. For sixteen years I thrived in my career. However, only a few years back I discovered I had ataxia, a rare neurological disease interrupting fine motor skills, causing hand tremors, lack of balance, and slurred speech. Upon being confined to a walking cane and losing my speech, my husband left me with two boys, where I had no way of financially providing for them. I remembered God's promise in Psalm 27: "My children will never beg for bread."

Words fail to express how God continues to provide for my family. My boys and I actually find it an exciting adventure every day watching how God is going to meet our next need. I'm overwhelmed by my God who provides. In one year I lost my address, my marital status, my health, and my occupation. But I did not lose God or my boys. Yes, fear often tries to creep in from time to time, but I remember: though fear might remain a lifelong challenge, God will always remain my lifelong Provider. Thank you, Jesus.

You can trust God with fears of the unknown. Why? *Because God provides.*

Heavenly Hosts in the Dark

I must be honest. One of my greatest fears when my children attended preschool revolved around me being the only adult in the home at night. After tucking myself in bed, I would hear every creaking sound from the backyard deck. My mind would race with thoughts of neighborhood bandits. I suppose that is why my favorite bedtime Bible story with Jason and Sara came from 2 Kings, about Elisha and his encounter with "visitors from above." The story goes like this.

Elisha and his servant lived in Samaria. The Scripture records how the servant awoke one morning to find their city besieged:

And behold an army of horses and chariots were circling the city. So the servant said, "Alas, my master! What shall we do?" Elisha replied, "Do not fear, for those who are with us are more than those who are with them." Then Elisha prayed for God to open the servant's eyes that he might see the unseen world of God's heavenly armies. And the Lord opened the servant's eyes and he saw the mountain full of horses and chariots of fire all around Elisha. —2 Kings 6:15-17

That incredible story still resounds in my soul and gives me goose bumps. Can you imagine seeing that? Glory to God. Yet the reality remains that, as heirs of salvation through Christ, we also can summon ministering beings around us. So as a single mom, I would pray:

Lord of Heavenly Hosts, I ask you to send your angels to 803 Glenn Drive to guard the four corners of my household. I ask that their protection stand in sacred service to You morning, noon, and night. Lord, You know I am a single mom, and I am afraid. Keep us from danger, and I will live in the realm of the invisible as I trust You by faith to protect us.

One time Sara sprinted into my bedroom at about four o'clock in the morning, calling, "Mommy, Mommy. Smoke!" We instantly followed our noses to her lamp. She had draped a sheet over it during the night, thinking the shaded light looked pretty. It had helped her fall asleep, but now it was about to go up in flames. *Something* awakened her out of a deep slumber. To this day I have no doubt in my mind what happened. My assigned angels hovered above, protecting our household.

Here is yet another example. A few days later, a rather handsome salesman rang my doorbell at about four o'clock in the afternoon. I ignored the bell. He left. That night a neighbor telephoned. "Pam, did you see the news? A man broke into the house up the street about 4:15." He must have left my home and gone directly to the other. Once again, my assigned angels labored above.

Friend, God promises to be with us. Calling out to Him summons His presence. It shifts our focus from fear to faith. In Psalm 56:1, David himself prayed, *"When I am afraid, I will trust in Thee."* Though it does not mean we will not have painful afflictions, it does mean that Satan's plan for permanent destruction will not prevail. God, the Lord of the Angel Armies, serves as our guardian and protector.

- *For the Lord your God is the Lord of lords, the awesome one who shields the cause of the fatherless and widows.*
  —Deuteronomy 10:17-19

- *And you shall say to the Lord, "My fortress, My God in whom I trust. And He will cover you with His pinions and under His*

wings you will take refuge. You will not fear the terrors at night
or even the destruction that lays waste at noon. And He will
order His angels to care for you and guard you where you go."
—Psalm 91

Yes, you can trust God with fears of the unknown. Why? *Because God protects.*

Go ahead. Pamper yourself. Envision the realm of the unseen, for He is the One who delivers. Pamper yourself. Lean on His bountiful provisions, for He is the One who provides. Pamper yourself. Relax in His care, for He is the One who sees. Give yourself permission to dote on you. Pamper yourself in God's wonder, and watch what happens to your fears.

Whispers from Jesus

I see your restless heart. But fear not, for I am beside you, in you. I'm speaking an anointing into your being: "Peace; be still." Feel the warmth of My care. When you forget Me as your protector, your mind drifts. Your worst-case scenario remains under My feet. Return to My promise to do something for you that you cannot do for yourself. You need not fear the future, for I am already there. When you feel afraid, hear My whisper, "I cherish you, My love."

Silent Reflection

1. What is your greatest fear of the unknown?
2. What keeps you from trusting God? Sin? Doubt? Fear? Worldliness? Explain.
3. Read Psalm 31. List the benefits of trusting in God.
4. Trusting is not giving God what you want but taking what He gives. Explain.
5. What will you take away from this chapter?

Gentle Respite for the Soul

God Gives Courage

Psalm 18:29—*With your help I can advance against a troop; with my God I can scale a wall.*

Deuteronomy 31:6—*Be strong and courageous; do not be afraid or* tremble at them, for the Lord your God is the one who goes with you. He will not fail you or forsake you.

God Provides Safety

Isaiah 43:1-3—*Do not fear, for I have redeemed you; I have called you by name; you are Mine! When you pass through the waters, I will be with you; and through the rivers, they will not overflow you. When you walk through the fire, you will not be scorched, nor will the flame burn you. For I am the Lord your God, the Holy One of Israel, your Savior.*

Proverbs 18:10—*The name of the Lord is a strong tower and the righteous runs into it and is safe.*

God Generates Abundance

Isaiah 58:11—*And the Lord will continually guide you, and satisfy your desire in scorched places, and give strength to your bones; and you will be like a watered garden and like a spring of water whose waters do not fail.*

2 Corinthians 9:10-11—*Now He who supplies seed to the sower and bread for food, will supply and multiply your seed for sowing and increase the harvest of your righteousness; you will be enriched in everything for all liberality, which through us is producing thanksgiving to God.*

CHAPTER THREE

From the Quagmire of Anger and Bitterness to Release through Forgiveness

Be quick to listen, slow to speak and slow to anger.
James 1:19

No other section in this book is more vital than this one. It is paramount. The freedom you long for, that lifestyle of spirit-filled wholeness and Christ-centered joy, flows out of that wondrous reservoir of God's love. He is ready to release the debilitating chains of anger and bitterness that bind you. The question remains: *Are you ready to participate with Him in the process?*

Six months after becoming a single mom, I attended a seminar about God's passion to set His children free. *Free? I thought. Me? Free? I want that!* However, while at the conference, I made a fool of myself. The teacher had the audacity to suggest that I forgive "a certain person" who had done me wrong by leaving our marriage. I stomped my foot, gave her a dirty look, and swished right out that door, leaving a trail of smoke behind me. While driving home, I kept my windows rolled up. I was *not* going to let my anger blow away like a feather in the wind.

Anger—Is It Ok?

Did you know that anger in and of itself is not a bad thing? It's a tool God has given us to respond to an injury or threat. As mothers, we understand. We wear an invisible sign around our neck: *If you hurt my child, you're dead meat by noon!* We're like the Canadian goose. If you get near her nest, she will nip you into a million pieces before the sun goes down.

Anger is something else, too. God uses it to motivate us to do what is right. Remember the day Jesus made headlines in the

Jerusalem Gazette for vandalizing the Temple square? Making a whip out of a cord, He drove out people and cattle, overturned the seats of the pigeon-dealers, and commanded, *"Take all this out of here and stop using my Father's house as a market."* Jesus didn't lose His temper. It was securely tucked away in His side pocket. His zeal exploded out of a righteous indignation regarding the Temple system. They were turning God's house into an outdoor Walmart. The Temple officials' disrespect for His Father stoked Jesus' fury.

Is it ok to be angry? Not only is it ok; it is normal. It is part of our emotional spectrum created by God. God's nature encapsulates love, holiness, and justice, yet He retains the capacity to experience anger. We bear His imprint. We get angry, too. God empathizes with our heartaches, understanding the reasons behind our anger. I hope that makes you feel better as a single mom.

If that's the case, then when does our anger that is "ok" become anger that is "not ok"? Paul instructed in Ephesians, "Be angry and sin not." I think Paul was directing that to me. I remember the time I asked my daughter's male Sunday-school teacher to follow my husband after work to find out where he was staying overnight. I did not like what he discovered. In fact, it threw me into a rage! Still fuming the next day, I loaded the kids in the backseat of the van, and we met their father in town. I pointed the van at his truck and revved the engine, ready to smash his vehicle to smithereens. Then I noticed the children peacefully sleeping in their car seats and snapped out of it. How could I put them in that situation?

It's amazing how foolish we mothers can be when we react to our frenzied emotions. In life we will collide head on with anger, but it's what we do with those fender benders that matters. Let's examine the culprits that lead to harmful, long-term anger.

Assaults of Every Kind

Many of you have been profoundly wounded, leaving you emotionally hemorrhaging with animosity. You have been cut to the quick. "Bitterness" comes from a word meaning "to prick." What an appropriate way to phrase it. You have been pricked, all right. You never dreamed you would find yourself in this predicament. What is the root of the offenses that cut you deeply and won't heal? Perhaps they originated from one of the following or a combination of them all.

A Broken Promise

Nothing hurts more than having someone you trust turning against you. Unfaithfulness is cruelty at the deepest level. King David was no stranger to personal offenses. He endured while his enemies railed against him. Note the intensity of his personal struggles:

Listen to my prayers, O God, do not ignore my plea. My thoughts trouble me and I'm distraught at the voice of my enemy. My heart is in anguish within me.

David continues to lament, revealing the source of his injury—a friend!

If an enemy were insulting me, I could endure it; if a foe were raising himself against me, I could hide from him. But it's you, a man like myself, my companion, my close friend, with whom I once enjoyed sweet fellowship as we walked together in the assembly of God's house.
—Psalm 55:12-14

In response to your own trials, you ask, *What? It's you—the one who vowed, "I do." What? It's you—the one who agreed to have children. What? It's you—the one who pledged, "I'll always love you." What? It's you? How could you?* Betrayal commits treason against the soul. Its crowning blow shocks you and then leaves you in a fog. Yet, hanging on to its injustice keeps you wedded to your offender through hatred.

Betrayal commits treason against the soul.

An Evil Plot

Nobody likes to look like a fool, especially Belinda, a single mom from Norman, Oklahoma.

I grew up a princess. I was the perfect child in our family, adopted, living a sheltered life at home, the sweet-girl type. In fact in high school I was voted "The Next Mother Teresa." Enough said. I married Tyson after I dated him nine months. He had two girls and we eventually had two of our own. Three years into our marriage, I discovered he was having an affair with a sixteen-year-old in our church youth group. Blaming me that I didn't give him the kind of sex he needed, he felt justified somehow. We separated but still tried to work it out.

But Tyson lived two different lives. He would invite his girlfriend and me to eat at the same restaurant at the same time with me unaware of the scheme, and he would go back and forth between tables seeing both of us. It was fun for the two of them to watch me innocently sit there not realizing what was happening. He'd play this little game at the drive-in, ball games, and even once at our home. When the two-year court battle began over the affair with the sixteen-year-old, I discovered more sexual abuse cases with an eleven- and twelve-year-old, along with his twelve-year-old cousin. I was married to a sexual predator, a master manipulator, and didn't know it. Now I'm left with two girls to raise alone. What happened to my Mother Teresa prediction?

A Personal Disregard

Rejection is a stinger, twisting to the nucleus of your self-esteem. This offense tells you, *Something is wrong with you. You are undesirable and defective. You don't measure up.* Friend, it hurts, doesn't it?

Do you remember the Bible character who became known as "the sister who was unloved by Jacob"? It was Leah, Rachel's oldest sister. Leah was married to Jacob, but it was Rachel whom he loved. I can't imagine the crushing affront to Leah when Jacob confessed that for years he had only loved her younger sister. How do you think that made Leah feel? She had given Jacob seven sons, but it was Rachel's silhouette that featured in his dreams. It was Rachel the "Bold and Beautiful" he craved, not Leah, the "Composed and Commonplace."

An Insensitive Comment

I continue to be stunned by others' lack of sensitivity. People just don't think! I will never forget attending my Sunday-school class a few weeks after my husband left (and yes, it was a married class, so I guess I was asking for it). A woman came to me with her own concerns: "My husband's going to Detroit for seven whole days, and I'll have the boys all by myself. Will you pray for me, Pam?" *Seriously?* I thought. *Seven days? My husband's gone forever, and you want me to pray for you?* I was already peeved that day, but her request sent me through the roof. I still remember the sting.

A Grotesque Mistreatment

Our office receives hundreds of letters from moms who have suffered physical or emotional abuse. In every story, the mom was humiliated or subjected to destructive behavior. Such incidents dissolve a single mom's sense of significance. Altercations often get out of hand: *"He choked me against the living-room wall in front of the kids."* Or, *"He chased me out the back door with an iron rod."* The result of such chaos is a family walking on eggshells. The children cower from the brutality while the mother seeks to numb the pain with alcohol, drugs, sex, shopping, or other vices.

These difficulties along with false accusations, physical injuries, and loss of financial resources writhe in your soul. Why do these vex you to your very marrow and breath? The answer might be difficult to swallow. Whether you deserved what happened or not, or want to admit it or not, you had an expectation. You didn't get what you wanted. Someone needs to fix it. Someone owes you something. You have been robbed. Do the following statements sound familiar?

- Jake, you took away the opportunity for us to work this out.
- God, you took away my children's daddy prematurely.
- Department of Human Services, you took away my daughter.
- Steve, you took away our original family unit.
- Brad, you took away my virginity and fled.
- God, you took away my perfect health.
- Kids, you took away the respect I deserved.

Ouch. Being stuck in the quagmire of bitterness, gasping for air, is not fun. I know. I've been there.

Let "Yet" Have Its Way

I have never met a single mom who preferred a pot of boiling, mean-spirited feelings to one of simmering contentment. Though some moms might enjoy hanging onto their boiling emotions for a while, none of them has ever admitted to desiring earthly repression over supernatural release. How about you? At what point are you ready to admit there's a problem with your anger? At what point are you ready to get rid of your exasperation? God holds the solution, but like a wild animal caught in a trap, are you ready to *yelp for help?*

I love David. He was a man after a single mother's heart. He, too, suffered disappointments of the gravest kind. It amuses me how he expressed his raw emotions to God. Remember earlier when we read how David's close companion betrayed him? Note what David said to God in his fury:

Yes, God. Haul my betrayers off alive to hell. Let them experience the horror, let them feel every desolate detail of a damned life.
—Psalm 55:15

Goodness, was he incensed! *Can I talk to God like that?* you wonder. God listens when we tell Him how we *really* feel. We might as well be honest with Him. He already knows. Yet, notice what David voiced to God immediately *after* He unloaded his anger. I love envisioning the Almighty on the edge of His throne, waiting to hear this next part.

Yet [it is implied], *I will call to God. He will help me. At dusk, dawn, and noon, I will sigh deep sighs. He will hear and rescue me in danger.*

"Yet"—that's it! Voicing a "yet" is that electrifying moment that determines your destiny: ruin or restoration. It is the fork in the road where you either take God's way or yours. It is that intentional choice to summon Heavenly forces to your cause rather than continue down the path of disintegration. "Yet" is the most powerful three-letter word ever spoken against the forces of darkness. Satan seeks to torment your soul. He waits to pounce when you are taking a spiritual nap; however, the moment Satan hears the word "yet," his scheme of mutilation unravels, and every evil plot assigned against you loses its power. You are not a prisoner in the enemy's camp. Why don't more single moms voice their "yets"?

Kingdom Authority

As a child of God, you are more than a sojourner passing through this life. You are authorized to enforce God's program in your household. You are it! You carry His scepter of the resurrected power of Jesus Christ, enabling you to break out of resentment and lead your family in righteousness.

When God commanded, "Be angry and sin not," He declared you have authority over your rollercoaster emotions. They don't control you. You control them. Remember David? He didn't play the tape in his mind concerning his misfortune. Rather, he expressed it to God. He called in the Heavenly Navy Seals—the "Yet" SWAT Team—leading his emotions away from mental obliteration toward spiritual liberation.

Friend, if you nurse and rehearse your injuries, your emotions follow suit. They lead to harsh inner chambers of withdrawal that cripples, retaliation that divides, impatience that crushes, angry outbursts that ruin, biting sarcasm that murders, and sins that shock even you. What kind of an existence is that? What kind of witness does that serve for your children? It is deadly to toy with bitterness. Is it any wonder that "anger" is one letter away from "danger"? The offense injured you deeply, but you have children to raise. Let them see Christ for who He is: conqueror, deliverer, overcomer, restorer, victor in a life that has been crushed by sorrows. Show them what "Jesus in skin" looks like. Who better to show them than you, their mother? What if you don't? Stark consequences follow every disobedience to God.

- You will forfeit the working of spiritual power and cut yourself short of God's favor. James 1:20 confirms, *"And be slow to stoking a hot heart because human anger does not achieve God's righteous purpose."*

- You will forfeit the promise of protection by affording the devil free play in your attitude and relationships. Ephesians 4:26-27 warns, *"Even if you're angry, do not sin. Never let the sun set on your anger or else you will give Satan a foothold."*
- You will forfeit the opportunity to be an effective witness. Hebrews 12:15 says the *"root of bitterness springing up causes trouble, and by it many defiled."*

Is it worth it? Remember anger's root? You didn't get what you wanted. Perform an about-face and change your "want." Express this to the Lord Most High:

- I *want* Your fortitude instead of my fickleness.
- I *want* Your power instead of my pettiness.
- I *want* Your love instead of my loathing.
- I *want* Your goodwill instead of my grudges.
- I *want* Your plan instead of my prejudices.
- I *want* Your tranquility instead of my tantrums.
- I *want* Your compassion instead of my cynicism.
- I *want* Your virtue instead of my vindictiveness.
- I *want* Your joy instead of my jealousy.
- Yes, God, that is what I *want*—all of You!

Prepare for the way of the Lord. The torrent of God's blessings swings open the golden gate of letting go. Give up the demand that the other person right the wrong that was done. How do you do that? Only one key unlocks the gate.

RELEASE THROUGH FORGIVENESS

Make a clean break with all cutting, backbiting, profane talk.
Be gentle with one another, sensitive. And forgive one another as
quickly and thoroughly as God in Christ forgave you.
Ephesians 4:32

I love single moms! As the difficulties of life take a toll on you, I come alongside as a friend with heartfelt compassion. God loves you far more than I do, and He, too, grieves when He sees His children mistreated or trapped in life's challenges. God is *for* you.

Is It Wrong?

I want you to meet two friends of mine.

Brittany's family history is riddled with one suicide after another. Her grandfather killed himself. His father killed himself. Her cousin killed himself. And then Daniel, her husband, killed himself, leaving her a widow with a four-year-old daughter. She inquires, "Is it wrong that I want my deceased husband to pay back what's been taken from us?"

Jeffery enlisted in the U.S. Navy. Though Amy, his wife, was not in favor of raising their daughters alone while he was deployed, she consented. He never returned. He preferred a lifestyle overseas without his family. Now their daughter Amanda is getting married. Amy inquires, "Is it wrong that I want my former husband to pay back what's been taken from us?"

Well, is it wrong? It is not wrong. However, where loss is involved, reimbursement is impossible. How can Daniel pay back the years that he missed being there for his daughter's dance recitals? How can Jeffery pay back the years that he missed tucking Amanda in bed at night? They are gone forever.

How about you? What outstanding debt remains tucked away in your thoughts of "if only things could have been different"? Friend, "hurt" is called "hurt" for a reason. There is an emotional component to it, where even an "I'm sorry" or "Here, take this money" won't erase the wrong. It is a painful reality to accept. You are waiting to be recompensed for something that can never be repaid. What is a mom to do? You have one of two options: either "forgive and forget," or "resent and remember." I know what you are thinking. You don't like either one of those choices!

Forgiveness—What Is It?

Many don't understand the biblical principles of forgiveness. Let's examine what it is *not*. It is *not* disregarding the seriousness of the offense or ignoring the heartache. It is *not* justifying the person's actions or placing them on the back burner, hoping time will heal the wounds. It is *not* forcing yourself to stomach the person by being all nice and sweet.

Forgiveness is a personal decision to get your heart right with

God. It is a resolution to move away from what feels natural. It is taking the offender off the hook of permanent blame but not off the hook of responsibility. As long as they are on your payback list, you are psychologically tied to them. When you transfer the penalty of the offense to God, you have given over ownership of the injustice. Forgiveness is canceling the debt owed and yielding the person to Him. It is refusing the temptation to penalize, get even, or denounce the transgressor. When the steroids of God's promises reduce the inflammation of anger, the damage takes on a new light. Forgiveness sets divine healing in motion.

Yet, I know what you are thinking: *I can't forgive this person. Doing so disregards my pain. It makes me feel as if my wounds don't matter. It minimizes the injustice, where it seems as though the other person suffers no consequences at all.* My friend, it's true. You are injured, but physical or emotional wounds should not deny you a forgiving heart. Forgiveness does not come out of your feelings, or none of us would ever get there. So where does it come from?

Forgiveness is birthed out of your will. Your negative emotions will run wild until you follow God's way. Don't ignore the significance of your "inside chooser"—your will. It is the route to recovery, demanding the decision to forgive your offender, not once, not twice, but unceasingly and without limits. Jesus taught that truth when he answered Peter's question, "Lord, how many times must I offer forgiveness?" Do you remember Christ's reply? "Forgive seventy times seven." Just as Christ unconditionally forgave us, we are called to do the same with others. By staying strong in the process of forgiveness, we achieve the victory our hearts long for.

Remember Brittany and her family tragedies with suicide? She testifies:

> *When I started the process of forgiveness and took down the barrier of resentment I'd erected between God and me, He removed the devil's seed of blaming others that fed my low self-worth and depression. I began to connect with my Father through prayer and reading His Word, and my desire to forgive changed. The process was worth the cost of not giving up. I praise God. Surrendering my will led to my God-ordained destiny—a free widow in Christ.*

The "See-to-It" Plan

As a single mom, you shoulder endless *external* responsibilities. You have to "see to" the laundry, "see to" the homework, "see to" the oil change. That should be your middle name—Mary "See-to-it" Jones. However, there is an *internal* "see-to-it" that far outweighs all the others combined. From it flows the energy to do all the rest. Observe Hebrews 12:15 again: "See to it *that no one falls short of the grace of God; that no root of bitterness springing up causes trouble, and by it many defiled.*"

See to it. That phrase means to guard against, to exercise oversight, to consider with caution. How seriously have you considered the snags of bitterness? Have you written your "See-to-it" plan to keep this foe at bay? How can these three questions fortify your strategy?

What If God Forgave You the Way You Forgive Others?

The parable about the merciless servant in Matthew 18 holds nothing back. No one has an excuse not to forgive his or her offenders—no one! In this story, a servant who owes an enormous sum of money begs the king to spare his life. The slave has incurred a financial debt he can never repay. The king pardons the lowly subject not only from death but from any penalty. He is a free man, ready to start a new life.

However, after his acquittal, the servant approaches a peer, chokes him, and demands repayment of a rather small sum. The friend begs for clemency, but the unwilling servant throws him into prison. When the king hears of the incident, he is outraged by the slave's ingratitude toward the pardon that had been extended to him.

The story parallels the truth: Jesus, the King, went to the cross to take our sin penalty upon Himself, a debt we can never repay. We are granted eternal life and absolved of our sins' penalty—past, present, and future. Yet, is it true that we won't forgive others in light of Jesus' sacrifice? The biblical drama concludes with a description of the king's attitude toward the ungrateful and ruthless servant: *"And the King was moved to anger, calling him a wicked slave."*

It is repulsive to God when we don't forgive our offenders. What dictates our decision to forgive? Is it the cross, or our feelings? What is keeping you from extending forgiveness to someone who has hurt you? Be honest.

- I am finding it difficult to forgive others. I have failed to yield to the cross's authority.
- I am viewing my offenses through the wrong filter. I have refused to acknowledge my own hardness of heart.
- I am trapped in a cycle of negativity, self-pity, and blame. I have neglected to confess bitterness for what it is: sin.

Perhaps we all need a clear reminder of the caustic nature of bitterness.

Who's Poisoning Whom?

Many embittered moms carry indignations of all sorts. They think they can live with them, grin and bear it. They cannot. Bitterness leaks. Ask the people around you. They might have the nerve to tell you the truth. On the other hand, they might not. No one likes to be in the line of fire of an active volcano.

Defending bitterness preserves a philosophy much like the little girl sitting on the bench in obvious agony:

"Little girl, what's wrong?" inquired a stranger.

"I'm sitting on a bumblebee," she replied.

The stranger continued, "Then why don't you get up?"

She snapped, "Because I figure it's hurting him more than it's hurting me."

Friend, two people suffer when you won't get off that bumblebee. Number one is you. How seriously have you considered why it's called "bitter"-ness? Why not "acidic"-ness? What does acid do to its container? Like acid, resentment eats away at your relationship with Christ. It poisons the spiritual compounds of a vibrant prayer life, causing you to fall short of God's best. It causes spiritual malnutrition by wilting your faith and dissolving Christ-generated hope and direction. Your witness becomes anemic, losing God's divine influence that sets the platform for prosperity. Most toxic of all, you lose intimacy with God. What is that worth to you? God has plans for you now. More importantly, He has plans for you later. One day your children will be grown and gone. What are you going to do then? Will you be at a place where God launches you into a more expansive sphere of service for His Kingdom because you chose obedience now? Will you let your "now," which feels like earthly boot camp in your spiritual training, serve as preparation for your "later"?

The bumblebee story is not done. Sitting on that bee stings someone else, too: your children (*"and by it many defiled"*). When someone is defiled they become involuntarily infected or polluted by an outside influence. What if I asked, "What do you want *most* for your children?" I know you would respond, "I pray they grow into healthy adults."

Friend, if you highlight any paragraph in this book, mark this one. My children are adults with babies. (Yes, I'm Grammy Pammy.) As I look back on my time as a single mother, I see I didn't do everything right, but I did some important things very well. My recent conversation with Jason and Sara stands out as a stunning revelation concerning the lifelong impact of our choices as mothers. They both agreed:

Mom, the greatest blessing you ever gave us was the gift of forgiveness to Dad. You extended to us the freedom to love him because he was our father. You didn't poison our lives with the pain you carried. We entered healthy marriages without baggage from the past.

Friend, *that* testimony alone remains reason enough to let go of an oppressive injustice. Let this moment serve as your benchmark of change. You must. It is critical.

Bitterness is the web that Satan spins to ensnare hapless prey. If you walked through a brown recluse cobweb, would you ignore the mesh clinging to your neck? Would you tolerate its fibers brushing your face? You would throw them off, fast. Friend, the enemy's web kills. Rip it off now, for your sake and your children's.

What If You Chose God's Reward?

God's Word promises in Proverbs 19:11, *"It is your glory to overlook an offense."* Good things come to those who obey God's

Word. Jesus longs to crown you with honor and respect. In God's economy, the greater the offense, the greater the opportunity for reward. When Christ returns to this earth, notice what He will bring with Him. Revelation 22:12 declares, *"My reward is with Me, to render to every man according to what he has done."* Friend, Jesus notices when you pass over a wrongdoing for His sake. With each choice to forgive, you lay up a treasure in your Heavenly reward basket.

In God's economy, the greater the offense, the greater the opportunity for reward.

Are you ready to yank out that root of bitterness? When you do, God drops a miracle seed in its place. I know about God's wonderwork. I am able to view my former husband and his wife in a hearty new light. They have served as my catalyst to press into God. Like a kaleidoscope, God has revealed His glorious beauty, which far surpasses the pain of any earthly divorce. Emotional wholeness and joy are the blessed recompense when Christ rules a heart.

Up, Up, and Away

When you feed off of your sufferings and injustices, you fail to take personal responsibility for your wellbeing. Do something about it. Move full speed ahead on that rollercoaster—onward and upward. Turn your eyes toward Jesus. Release every appendage of bitterness and enjoy the ride. Let your "See-to-it" plan take the lead.

Clarify the Debtors

Make a list of any person in your liability directory whom you need to forgive. Is it the father of your children? Is it someone from a former relationship? Is it God? Could it even be you? Dig deep and ask, "Who makes me *wrinkle up* on the inside?"

Cancel the Debt

Determine by the choice of your will to discharge every transgressor.

Thank you, Lord, for dying on the cross and extending Your forgiveness to me. As an act of my will I forgive (name) and take (him or her) off my emotional hook and place (name) on Your hook. Though (name) hurt me greatly, I terminate this offense and forgive (name) as You have forgiven me. Amen.

Case Closed

Dismiss the temptation to hash out an altercation all over again. Submit it to God's authority.

> *Forget.* Philippians 3:13 encourages, *"Forgetting those things which are behind, press on."* Forget means "to no longer care about, to no longer remain harmed by." Practice forgetfulness.
> *Feast.* Enjoy making Jesus happy. Philippians 2:13 notes *"God is at work in you both to will and work for His good pleasure."* Practice delighting God.
> *Focus.* Philippians 4:8 says *"Whatever is honest, just, pure, lovely and has a good report, think on these things."* Practice this mindset. *As my thinking goes, so goes my entire being.*

We get to pick. Will you choose "forgive and forget" or "resent and remember"? Precious friend, remove the veil of contention. Do away with the quarrelsome spirit. Eliminate the desire to retaliate. Get rid of every residue of anger and bitterness. God longs to set you free, but how can He heal you if He can't reach you?

Whispers from Jesus

There is no greater obstacle to My presence than bitterness. If it angers you, then it conquers you. Beloved, I was there when the offense took place. It hurt Me, too. But it cannot define the way you live or view your future. Release it. I have called you to walk away from what has happened to you so I can work in you. When you feel angry, hear My whisper, "I cherish you, My love."

Silent Reflection

1. Five assaults were listed early in the chapter. Does one fit you?
2. When have you "nursed and rehearsed" an offense?
3. Bitterness is prolonged anger seeking some form of revenge. Explain.

4. True or false: your "will" determines the direction of your destiny.
5. Summarize Ephesians 4:31-32.

Gentle Respite for the Soul

Forgiving Others

Mark 11:25—*When you stand praying, if you hold anything against anyone, forgive him, so that your Father may forgive you.*

Romans 12:16-17—*Live in harmony with one another. Do not be overcome with evil, but overcome evil with good.*

Matthew 5:23-24—*If therefore you are presenting your offering at the altar, and there remember that your brother has something against you, leave your offering there before the altar and go your way; first be reconciled to your brother, and then come and present your offering.*

Forgiving Yourself

Acts 13:38-39—*In Jesus there is forgiveness for your sins. Everyone who believes in Him is freed from all guilt and declared right with God.*

Daniel 9:9—*The Lord is merciful and forgiving, even though we have rebelled against Him.*

Ephesians 1:7—*In Him we have redemption through His blood, the forgiveness of our trespasses, according to the riches of His grace.*

CHAPTER FOUR

From the Jitters of Anxiety to Resting in God's Peace

An anxious heart weighs a man down.
Proverbs 12:25

When I was speaking at a conference for single moms in Tennessee, Melanie stood out from the other attendees. She looked seriously troubled, her eyes tense with pain. I wondered a few times if she was breathing or just numbed by the words of truth being imparted to her. During the break, I rushed to help her. Entrapped and unaware, Melanie had fallen prey to an overtaxed schedule as a single mom. Her survival dangled in midair, swaying between a present state of restlessness and a future state of uncertainty. One might diagnose this condition as *a-n-x-i-e-t-y!* She was anxious, all right, obsessed with the load of managing her household of four children while attempting to make peace with her past. Does that sound familiar?

Earthquake Jitters

I read about an eight-year-old girl in Southern California who suffered from an ailment that kept her awake half the night. She would quiver and shake at the slightest notion. Even some adults in the area were afflicted by similar symptoms. The common denominator was apprehension over the unpredictability of the next earthquake and was triggered by the dilemma of having neither a place to hide nor a person to save them.

It reminds me of a few single moms I know. They suffer from similar "quake jitters," the fear of unexpected upheavals with no season of relief in sight and nobody to come to their rescue. Thoughts of the next burden contribute to their stress until, finally, they are drained of emotional and physical reserves. No wonder *single motherhood is hard!*

Anxiety is your body's normal response to stressful thoughts and circumstances. It becomes harmful when it interferes with daily life. As tension between the plates builds up for an earthquake, excessive worry pressuring the soul frustrates its quest for peace. You know full well what emotional overload feels like. It is a persistent tension between your heart and mind about something that you can't fix. It comes from confusion and bustle that gnaw away at your sanity. If left unattended, it festers, creating critters more destructive than termites. It breeds worrymites! And worrymites don't just nibble; they smother and devour their prey. How appropriate, as the root word for worry means "to choke." As a single mom, don't you sometimes feel as if you are being *strangled* by the daily pressure of:

- parenting the children?
- working two jobs?
- taking care of yourself?
- dealing with loneliness?
- mowing the lawn?
- tripping over the Legos?
- sorting the dirty laundry?
- energizing the bedtime Bible stories?

Goodness, no wonder you are overwhelmed while your best functioning abilities remain stuck on, *"Help me, God. Help me!"*

Mother Nature

I am intrigued by the term *"mother* nature." Why isn't it *father* nature or *cousin* nature? It's obvious: motherhood serves as one of the greatest forces in this universe. It is the mother who carries the child in the womb. It is the mother who nurses the baby. Being a mother is one thing. Being a single mother is something quite different.

I will never forget the day in the park when, as a brand-new single parent, I realized something. *Ok, God. It's You and me now. We are the only "parents" under the roof.* Although I felt His presence like never before, *I* would be the one answering Jason and Sara's questions about why their daddy was gone. *I* would be the one humming "Jesus Loves the Little Children" as I rocked them into dreamland. *I* would be the one tending to the midnight screams when their back molars broke the surface. *I* would be the one! Talk about being overcome by mental distress and exhaustion. I didn't know how I could parent on the outside and mend my broken heart on the inside.

- How would I handle seeing the children's dad with another woman at Jason's soccer games?
- How would I redefine the holidays and do away with ten years of marital Christmas traditions?
- How would I leave the married department at church and traipse into the singles department?

You, too, have a stash of *how would I* questions tucked in the inner lining of your survival kit. The very nature of these fears throws you into suffocating apprehension, where it is easier to live in a state of unrest than to breathe. Why is this? The solo-parent life doesn't feel natural. When you sat on Santa's lap, you never asked him if you could be a single mom. You never asked the tooth fairy to grant you motherhood without a spouse. You never asked for the tattoo on your forehead: *W* for widowed, *D* for divorced, or the scandalous *U* for unwed.

These images create an emotional wilderness in your heart. Regardless of the invisible scarlet stamp on your brow, you are forced to press on. You are a single mother. There is work to do, parent/teacher conferences to attend, and spiritual lessons to employ. You have no choice but to keep moving with one courageous stride after another, while somehow learning to manage it with dignity and charm. After all, the kids are watching, remember? Friend, you have to suck it up and deal with it.

I recall one of my unwanted "deal with it" realities. I did not like it at all. It always threw me into an agonizing whirl that took me days to recover from. I dreaded it. Did you hear me? *I dreaded it!*

The Grim Switch

Every two weeks, I met my former husband at a halfway point

to transfer the kids for the weekend. Though I found a few days without the children a revitalizing breather, a respite with a sprinkle of "me" time, I often spent the weekend crying my eyes out. I still loved this tall, dark, and handsome man, and laying eyes on him during the big switch thrashed my soul. I thought, *Pam, don't look at him and you'll be fine. Let Jason and Sara out of the car, keep your head down, kiss 'em goodbye, and drive off. Fast!*

The Lord gave me a plan to help me in my distress, and—glory to God—it worked. While approaching the parking lot to hand over the children, I would play my favorite Christian song and the very presence of Jesus would well up in my gray minivan, carrying me on eagle's wings until I drove away. Heaven itself invaded my vehicle, where angels performed a dance recital in my heart, ushering me back to the house (or was it the mall?). But something happened one day, an incident that cut me like a chainsaw.

"Mommy, Mommy," Jason chirped from the backseat as I pulled into the parking lot. "Mommy, there she is. Come meet daddy's girlfriend."

Recoiling as though splashed by cold water, I lashed back in my mind, *Over my dead body!*

"Mommy, Mommy," his cheerful voice entreated, his heels digging into the grass while he pulled me out of the car. What was I to do? Make a scene? I tried with all my motherly might to scoot him on his way and leave me alone for the time being. Yet, with the stubborn enthusiasm of a five-year-old, he insisted that I meet *our* new family friend.

I succumbed. Emerging from the car in dazed slow motion, I whispered, "Ok, Jesus. Where are you?" Meanwhile, a tall woman stepped out of the Bronco. She was ten years younger than me (naturally), with nary a curl in her lovely blonde locks. I discovered I had been her counselor at Kanakomo/Kanakuk Camps. Her nickname was Rabbit, and we had been pen pals. I had adored this little camper, and *she* would be my children's stepmother one day. Friend, I didn't know whether to hug her or hit her! Was I anxious? You bet. Was I overwhelmed? You bet. Was I angry? You bet.

What is a mom to do when she has been splattered on the

concrete in one of those anxious moments? You know those times in your own life when your heart stops dead in its tracks:

- What? You have been sexually molesting our five-year-old daughter?
- What? A car hit my husband on a motorcycle, and he is not breathing?
- What? You want to live with your dad and his girlfriend?
- What? You're taking my kids away because of my anger issues?
- What? I'm not your girlfriend anymore even though my kids call you Daddy?

These shocking moments leave you paralyzed from horror, reeling in a state of anguish. They pursue you as a ravenous cat runs down a mouse. Yet when the chase is over, you are back at square one, faced with this gruesome reality: you *alone* are left to *deal with it.*

Pitbulls' Bite

It was a sunlit afternoon when I took my children on a nature walk in their little red wagon. We passed by a yard with a sign that read: *Pitbull Puppies Bred Here.* I got the message. My kids and I would *not* be trespassing to give those pups doggie treats. Although I couldn't see the dogs, I knew danger loomed behind that backyard gate.

Your destructive, rollercoaster emotions as a single mom resemble that sign for all to view: *Overwhelmed—Anxiety Bred Here!* Behind that gate looms pitbull dangers, realities that devour every opportunity Christ offers for a life of purposeful joy. Like a snowball gaining speed and growing bigger as it rolls, your anxiety gains momentum and grows larger with worries. I learned a principle as a single mother that saved me many days of prolonged despair: *Pam, if you don't give God what is bothering you today, tomorrow you will feel ten times worse.*

Friend, anxiety not only barks but bites, leaving deep wounds. What are the hazards of feeding this animal morsels of daily fretfulness?

Anxiety's Ramifications

Persistent anxiety leads to consequences. Though you might think worrying serves only as a minor malady, its damage bleeds into other parts of your being. There remains a unique relationship between physical disorders and emotional contributors. For example:

- If you are stressed about the holidays, your anxiety could increase blood pressure and cause shortness of breath, chest pain, and fatigue.
- If you are taxed by the sheer number of your obligations, it might affect brain chemistry, causing temporary memory loss or an increase in irritability.
- If you are frazzled about your new transition, career, or upcoming decision, it might interfere with your adrenal system, in which case, the more carbs you eat, the heavier you get and the worse you feel.

Prolonged anxiety affects our wellness in multiple ways. In the severest of cases, anxiety left unchecked and compounded by Satan's lies can cause delusional thoughts. This fact reminds me of Jenny. Our ministry met her at our single moms' conference. Suffering from a lack of motivation, she collapsed under chronic anxiety brought on by feelings of guilt. When she entered the building of our event, she had suicide in mind and was grasping for the last straw of hope: *I'll go to this conference. If it doesn't help, I'm taking my life before Monday morning.* She meant it, too!

What happened to push Jenny to this limit? How could she overlook her inborn survival instinct and disregard her six-month-old son, foreclosing every possibility of future happiness? How could the pain of her dying trump the pain of her living? There is an easy answer. Intense anxiety clouds judgment and warps one's perception of what is real. It imposes grave penalties if left unattended. Never underestimate the dangers of living with anxiety. *Anxiety multiplies.*

On a side note, Jenny surrendered her life to Jesus that Friday evening and today testifies of the power of Christ to bolster a single mother's weary soul. God promises a way out of anxiety's terror.

Haggard Hand-Me-Downs

Every single mom loves it when a friend gives her a surprise. One day Stacy gave Jennifer a gift of clothes her son had outgrown. However, when Jennifer opened the box, the trousers had a rip in the lining and there were Clorox stains everywhere. With eyebrows drooped, she considered the situation: *Oh, well, I'll just turn the pants inside out. No one will know they're tainted.* There is a hidden lesson in this little story.

Great mothers adopt a mom mission statement that defines their values about childrearing. Mine is this: *the greatest gift to give your child is a godly example.* In other words, modeling matters. Nothing takes the place of a mother who sets the standard of Christ-likeness for the children to emulate. "But I can't do that all the time," you say. You don't have to be a perfect mom to be an effective witness. Our success or failure in modeling does not depend upon whether or not our performance is impeccable. Its success depends on a mom's purposeful decision to allow Christ to live through her, especially when she feels weak and inadequate. Your legacy leaves behind the best of you, igniting the greatest in your children.

In 1 Corinthians 11:1, Paul exhorts, *"Be imitators of me as I am of Christ."* In other words, "Model me as I am modeling Jesus." How many of us exhibit that kind of mindset with our children? You have a genuine opportunity to show your kids the beauty of what it looks like to live under the influence of God's power and Word. I know many healthy children who live in a household with a single mother at the helm. That mother is no different from you. She juggles a hefty weight of responsibilities, too. However, she has found the secret that empowers her role modeling: "No soiled 'hand-me-down examples' in this home. If my children are going to see Jesus, they will have to see Him in me."

When a mom doesn't live by these standards, she is vulnerable to her adverse emotions. Friend, your children will someday speak about what they remember from their formative years. What will they say about the atmosphere you provided? Was it a place of love, patience, and self-control, even though you personally struggled? Or will they say, "Mother lived on the edge; she was cranky and always agitated about *something.* I was glad to graduate from high school and get out of the house."

So beware of the long-term damages of stress and be careful not to rip the lining or drop Clorox on your child's wellbeing by modeling poorly. And whatever you do, don't send them to school with their "emotional trousers" turned inside out. *Anxiety taints.*

Spiritual Infertility

A parable portrays a story about a behavior that is either pleasing or displeasing God. My favorite parable of Jesus revolves around the sower in Matthew 13, where the seed of God is tossed on four types of soil, each one representing a man's heart. The third one captures my attention. How would that read in the *Single Mother Bible Version? "And the words of Jesus were sown onto the single mom's heart, and she heard the words, but worries about her children and her lost dream choked the peace that Christ offered, and she became spiritually barren and unproductive."*

What makes a mom spiritually fruitless? I witnessed an incident in a donut shop that reminded me of that question. I was treating my toddlers to a morning feast of donut holes with chocolate sprinkles. Another mother's two-year-old son began choking next to us, his face turning a reddish purple. We both rushed to his aid like in-house physicians. Permanent brain damage or even death loomed before us. Choking is a serious matter. Fortunately, the boy was ok.

God's Word cautions that when we worry, we choke our relationship with Christ. We allow a foreign object to lodge in our spiritual windpipe and block the flow of Christ's life and oxygen for a well-ordered life. We are left helpless, for earth's 911 operator cannot rescue us. This makes us a perfect afternoon snack for Satan.

My daddy was a gardener. I watched him labor over plucking weeds, creating a more spacious environment for his plump tomatoes. Our lives are like his garden: we have the potential to produce spiritual fruit, as well as thistles of every kind. Hope dies when we focus more on the poisonous wildflowers and thorns than on God's promises. Friend, if you are fixated on your anxieties, expect them to do what they were created to do: grow like weeds. They will take for themselves what the "good" plant needs: moisture, nourishment, sunlight.

I am convinced that we are much too relaxed and *uncomfortably comfortable* with stressing out, thinking that we cannot escape it. But we can. In John 14:1, Jesus instructed, *"Do not let your heart be troubled."* Rather, keep it in the *"Sonlight."* He knew something we didn't concerning our wellness.

Worry:

- impedes our progress toward wholeness.
- curbs our craving to read God's Word.
- chokes our lifeline of hope.
- dehydrates our witness.
- steals our enjoyment of blessings.
- soils our longing to pray.
- snips our joy.
- shapes our future.

Above all, worry short-circuits our yearning to sit at Jesus' feet. Remember Christ's words to Martha as she stewed in the kitchen over something as trifling as pots and pans? "Martha. Martha. You are so uptight. You are missing the better part. I am here."

What if He probed, "Pam. Pam. You are so tied in knots. You are missing the help I came to give. I am here." What if I responded, "Well, Lord, to be honest, I don't believe You are capable of handling this. Though I am turning a reddish purple, it's necessary that I worry about these 'pots and pans' of mine." The farther we drift along the paths of anxiety, the less aware we are of God's presence. Bottom line: at all times, *anxiety chokes.*

I wonder what would happen if we envisioned our anxieties squeezing out God's better part. How can we move from fretting and unbelief to abiding in God's rest?

RESTING IN GOD'S PEACE

You will stay in perfect peace to the extent that you trust in Him.
Isaiah 26:3

It used to soothe my heart as a single mom when someone said,

"Pam, just rest in God's peace." I tried. However, the comfort only lasted about two minutes until the next thought barged in: *Well, how do I do that?*

What does it look like to abide in that undisturbed place of repose? And how do you stay there when the teacher tells you, "Your daughter made an F in geometry," or your heart cries, "I want a mate by Valentine's Day"? In your daily affairs, how do you find that balance between peace and harmony on God's side and trust and confidence on your side? Do you need God to blow you a kiss? Do you need the edge taken off of your worries? How do you thrive in the center of *God's calm?* Here is a beginner's peace guide for single moms in four easy steps.

Step One: Roll It Back

A single mom from Tennessee shared the battle cry of many single mothers' plight concerning their children:

I feel so responsible for everything and everybody. If I didn't work, they'd starve. If I didn't guide, they'd fall. If I didn't pray, they'd faint. It's all up to me, me, me!

While the initial choice to release yourself from the burden is your own, in reality, it is not all up to *you, you, you*. It is a matter of ownership. Who owns the children? Who owns the burden? If it is you, then you are in trouble, and you will never experience God's tranquility. If it is Him, you need to "play ball."

When Jason and Sara were young, I did what most moms do with their toddlers. During playtime I rolled a beach ball back and forth to them on the floor. I had possession of the ball. Then they had possession. God wants us to "play ball" but leave the ball with Him. In Psalm 55, David confirmed God's heart as a ball player seeking teammates. *"Cast your burden upon the Lord and He will sustain you."* The Hebrew word for "cast" means "to roll back onto." I love that analogy. You have a specific place to lay your burdens: on the Almighty's shoulders. However, what happens when you take the offer, roll the affliction onto Him, and still feel the burden? How do you ignore the heartaches that won't go away?

"Casting" involves developing a different relationship with your burden. It is the notion of comradeship. You place the disappointments on God's right shoulder, where He carries the responsibility for both its outcome and your emotional and spiritual care. You place yourself on His left shoulder, where you come alongside as a witness and prayer partner. It is impossible to totally disassociate yourself from the astronomical cargo you carry, but you can shift the ownership to Him. You are a single mom. But who is He? He is a single dad, making the two of you a fine couple. When you plop yourself onto Him, companionship lightens the load. God has a greater plan concerning your avalanches. It is not to remove them on the spot, though He might. It is to teach you to lean on Him while they are coming. It is developing a dependent perspective, the opposite being: *I'll just handle this myself.* Humble reliance engenders a peaceful trust in God's abundant strength. Christ bears you up when you are facing disheartening realities, such as:

- My preschooler struggles because her classmates all have dads at home. She doesn't.
- The foster agency called. I'm not getting custody of Amanda.
- Father's Day is tomorrow. That's my hardest day of the year.

When life throws you curveballs, roll them back onto Jesus. David's Psalm concludes with a victory shout: *"And you* shall not *be shaken."* Did you hear that? Glory, glory, I love those two words: *"shall not."*

Step Two: Fill 'Er Up

Being indwelt and filled with the Holy Spirit serves as a key factor in overcoming anxiety. When Jesus ascended to His Father, God sent the Holy Spirit, a spiritual-life navigator, to point us to Jesus' teachings and His promise to come alongside us in the Christian life. The Spirit adorns us with Christ-like virtues called the fruit of the spirit: love, joy, *peace,* patience, kindness, goodness, faithfulness, gentleness, and self-control. These "graces" that reside in every believer stand by as vigilant friends, waiting to be activated. *Then why am I fretting about my child-support payment and worrying about my teenager? How can I experience that peace?* you ask.

Abiding in these graces requires the Holy Spirit's assistance. When you gave your life to Jesus, you received the Holy Spirit, always having access to Him. But the question remains: does He always have access to you? Perhaps you are like me. Sometimes the Spirit doesn't have all of my attention. What does it look like to let the Holy Spirit take charge when we temporarily drift? Recently while driving to Walmart, I almost ran out of fuel. Thank Heaven I noticed the red light on my dashboard. Just as I had to physically stop and refill my tank with gas, when I am spiritually low, I have to stop and ask the Spirit to refuel my tank with His gas. Friend, when you are running on fumes, recharge! The Holy Spirit is waiting to fill 'er up, and not only the tank but the entire vehicle: the glove compartment, the front seat, the trunk. He works to permeate every square inch of your "car" with his presence: your consciousness, choices, words, and actions.

Do you feel overburdened? Are you running on empty with a low peace tank? Stop and ask the indwelling Holy Spirit to fill you with His presence.

Lord, I need You. My peace remains buried under this albatross I am carrying. I am hungry and thirsty for Your fullness. Replenish me with Your Spirit. In Jesus' name, I declare a cease-fire from my anxious thoughts. I relinquish my will and give You complete control. Empower me according to Your promises, as I claim the richness of Your provisions by faith. Thank you for Your peace, coming to life in and through me. I receive it at this moment. In Christ's name, amen.

Friend, you cannot yield control to the Holy Spirit and nurse anxiety at the same time. Only one gets to ride on your rollercoaster. Which one will you choose?

You cannot yield control to the Holy Spirit and nurse anxiety at the same time.

Step Three: Pray and Give Thanks

He emerged from the pages of Scripture after the resurrection of Christ. If ever a Bible character had reason to live in a state of perpetual fret, it was this man. He too endured hardship. Three times he found himself beaten with rods and shipwrecked, surviving against all odds with third-degree burns of mental anguish. His name was Paul. In the depths of his emotional and physical peril, he discovered God's remedy for anxiety. His letter to the Philippian church brought encouragement.

Philippians 4:6-7 says, *"Be anxious for nothing but in everything by prayer and supplication with thanksgiving let your requests be made known to God and the peace of God which surpasses all understanding shall guard your hearts and minds in Christ Jesus."* What was God saying to the believers in Philippi? If Paul had addressed the same letter to you, perhaps he would have transcribed the following from Jesus:

Dear Single Mom,

Don't be uptight about anything. Let go of feeling that "it" wasn't fair. Let go of fuming over what happened. Let go of wishing your life could be different. Let go of wanting a husband when you have Me. When you analyze a circumstance more than you analyze My faithfulness, it brings on a spell of anxiety and discontent. I enable you to think otherwise. You have alternatives when you are stuck in the cycle of despair. Recognize your agonizing and stop it. Pray instead. It dispels rampant fears and brings My presence and solution into the problem. I create a mood of emotional calm around you. Talk to Me. Tell Me how you feel, what you need. Communing with Me weakens anxiety's DNA. It releases the angst of obsessing and transfers your burdens to a higher Source.

And give thanks. Thankfulness guides your heart from unbelief in My faithfulness to peace in the guarantee of My provisions. Your grateful heart opens the window for My light. I am your peace. I garrison your heart, placing a shield over it that thwarts the enemy's fiery darts.

Beloved mom, when I left this earth I entrusted you with an official document, My "Last Will and Testament." Do you know what I willed to you as a single mother? My peace. Have you cashed it in? Are you enjoying its benefit, or are you throwing it away to your greatest enemy: worry? I send My love message: "I've got it covered, My dear. Do not be anxious."

Jesus

Friend, God's peace is found in *Christ* alone. Even if you found the man of your dreams and inherited a mansion on Mt. Everest, anxiety would find you. Gird yourself for action against this tormentor by implementing God's dynamic duo: prayer and giving thanks. You have the peace of God to protect you, the promises of Jesus to instruct you, and the presence of the Holy Spirit to guide you.

Step Four: Call in the Cops

We have learned thus far that abiding in God's peace requires (1) letting go of managing our emotions by casting them upon the Lord's shoulder, (2) asking for the Holy Spirit's power, and (3) living in an atmosphere of prayer and thanksgiving. What is step four?

Our battle with anxiety will continue until we see Christ. Until then, God has given us a way to cut off worry's ambush and the destructive patterns in our thinking. It comes from the ongoing process of employing God's ways over ours. Thoughts that don't envelop the faithfulness of Christ serve as foreign intruders to our soul. They need to be treated like burglars: captured, handcuffed, marched to God's throne for judgment, stripped of their power, and ordered to defer to Christ. We were not wired to worry. God designed us to "house" in His peace, so why do we tolerate such thoughts in our own houses? How can we police our thoughts, monitor the P.U.L.S.E. of our qualms, and wield our *Jesus Power?* Conquest follows a strategy.

P = Pinpoint the thought. Start thinking about what you are "thinking about." When you spot a thought that is leading you away from God, call it out by name: *Fear, come out in Jesus' name.* When you exercise your authority, destructive emotions come under your control.

U = Unload the thought's venom. Release your adverse emotions to God. Tell Him how the thought made you feel. When you fail to express it to God, it leaves the pain in the darkness and gives anxiety its strength. Bring Jesus, the Light of the world, into the equation.

L = Look for the thought's root. Dig below the surface. *Why am I anxious? What is triggering this emotion? Is this bigger than God? Is it* strong enough to destroy me or my children? Let your perception be reshaped by God's Holy Word.

S = *Stand* on the truth. Break out of worry's destructive game. Speak with conviction, even if you don't feel like it: "I am *not* overwhelmed. I am *not* ruined. I possess God's risen power." When you verbalize Christ's words, it cleanses your mind and breaks the stronghold.

E = *Expect* a change. Transformation follows faith. Believe it and know that you are being altered by praying, "By God's Holy Spirit I am being renewed." Proverbs 23:7 says that as a man thinks in his heart, so he *is*. You act out of the sum of your thoughts, so add each one carefully.

The solution to the gnawing pest of anxiety remains quite clear. Follow God's way, not your way.

> *And now may the Lord of peace Himself give you*
> *peace at all times and in every way.*
> 2 Thessalonians 3:16

Whispers from Jesus

I see your restless heart. At the cross I not only bore your sins, but I bore your mental anguishes so you wouldn't have to carry them. When you dwell on the unsettled matters more than Me, you lose confidence in My faithfulness. Do not measure the demands of your day against your own stress, for I am with you. When you feel anxious, hear My whisper, "I cherish you, My love."

Silent Reflection

1. What are your "deal with it" realities?
2. Of the three types of anxiety's ramifications, which one spoke to you? Why?
3. Four steps for abiding in God's peace were provided. Summarize each one.
4. Dwelling on the things of God reshapes your living and thinking. Expand on that truth.
5. Read Isaiah 26:3. What is the condition for staying in God's perfect peace?

Gentle Respite for the Soul

God Sees Anxiety

1 Peter 5:6-7—*Humble yourselves, therefore, under the mighty hand of God, that He may exalt you at the proper time, casting all your anxiety upon Him because He cares for you.*

Psalm 37:7—*Be still before the Lord and wait patiently for him. Do not fret when men succeed in his ways, when they carry out their wicked schemes.*

God Gives Reassurance

Psalm 121:1-2—*I will lift up my eyes to the mountains, from whence comes my help. My help comes from the Lord who made heaven and earth.*

Psalm 43:5—*Why are you in despair, O my soul, and why are you disturbed within me? Hope in God for I shall again praise Him for the help of my countenance, and my God.*

God Grants Peace

John 14:27—*Peace I leave with you; My peace I give to you; not as the world gives, do I give to you. Let not your heart be troubled, nor let it be fearful.*

Colossians 3:15—*And let the peace of Christ rule in your hearts, to which indeed you were called in one body, and be thankful.*

CHAPTER FIVE

From the Wilderness of Loneliness to Practicing God's Presence

When my father and mother forsake me, the Lord will take care of me.
Psalm 27:10

I surveyed more than two thousand single moms about their top three negative emotions. Is it any surprise that 90 percent of the responses included loneliness? There is nothing more painful. You can easily peg a lonely woman when you hear these words: "No one understands what I'm going through or what it's like to be me." That persistent feeling of alienation is an emotional disease, a pathological condition stemming from the most basic human needs: feeling valued and included. I recall the sense of disconnectedness in our family unit every Christmas Eve when I took Jason and Sara to the church service alone. I imagine I am not the only one who has experienced this feeling.

God's Remote Hall of Fame

Why is it that notable men and women in the Bible found themselves enrolled in the undergraduate school of reclusiveness? Why would God allow those He loves to endure such distress? From Genesis to Revelation, God's Word stands as a document full of people who encountered loneliness.

- Moses was a leader. After he wandered for forty years in the wilderness, God didn't allow him to enter into the Promised Land with his people. How do you think Moses coped the night after everyone left?
- Solomon was a king. This man of royalty earned the reputation of being the wisest and richest leader in the

East. Yet Ecclesiastes portrays him as a sad ruler. How do you think Solomon felt reigning from a castle glazed with gold, suffering from a forlorn heart?

- Eve was the first woman. In the cool of the day, she walked in perfect fellowship with God. When she introduced sin into the world, God removed His presence. How do you think Eve reacted the second His Spirit departed?

Countless other biblical heroes—Paul, David, Peter, and more—suffered from alienation. However, the enduring champion of champions remains Jesus Christ, the Messiah, who placed the weightiness of *all* loneliness for *all* time on His shoulders at the cross. Jesus not only bore our sins in His body, but He took upon Himself the entire range of our emotions so that we would not have to bear them alone. Jesus understands loneliness. He suffered the ultimate separation by being alienated from His Father on that cross. Christ overcame the wound of loneliness for one reason: so that it could no longer inflict itself on us.

Loneliness—What Is It?

Genesis 2:18 says, *"And the Lord discerned, 'It is not good for man to be alone. I will make a helper suitable for him.'"* The original word for "alone" means "isolated."[1] In other words, "It is not good for man to be *isolated* in and of himself." What happens when we don't foster relationships with others?

In your case (excluding mothers who have adopted children or others who found themselves in a one-night romance), being alone remains a difficult challenge because, previously, you enjoyed the companionship of a significant other. That makes the single life all the more problematic. Every holiday or song brings back memories of thriving as a couple, so that the adjustment to a solitary lifestyle feels awkward. It creates a barren soul, making it uncomfortable to communicate with peers and hampering the aspiration to make new friends. One single mom conveyed her frustration to me: *"When my relationship with my spouse broke apart, my desire to socialize went away with my wedding ring."* Is it any wonder that single moms fall prey to depression, codependency, parental guilt, blame, or loss of self-worth and enthusiasm? Another single mother expressed to me her problem with isolation: apathy. *"I'm unproductive. Why bother? And besides, who cares?"* That is the danger of emotionally throwing in the towel: the less you do, the worse you feel.

Loneliness hurts. As a separated wife, I attended my husband's mother's wedding (on a side note, aren't weddings painful to attend?). I still hoped that my husband and I would get back together, so I joined the celebration. However, when it was time for the family picture, I didn't know if I should get in it or not. What if we got back together in years to come, and I wasn't in the photograph? So I mustered up enough courage to walk onto that stage, and guess what? "Someone" told me to sit back down.

I know the pregnancy of loneliness and the babies it delivers: denunciation, fury, and being branded as a loser. Humiliation pummels the spirit. Maybe you have been degraded to the core. King David understands. In Psalm 25:16, he grappled with the heaviness of life in the face of his trouble and troublemakers: "Lord, look at me and help me. I'm all alone and in big trouble." Friend, when your soul is in protest, it feels like *big trouble!*

Toxic Triplets

Although you cannot escape your predicament, you can follow God's Word and the advice of professionals who have guided thousands of single mothers through the wasteland of unhealthy emotional withdrawal. You can't just shake it off, but you can avoid its long-term damage. Three dangerous consequences trail the ravages of loneliness: neediness, jealousy, and temptation. Each exhibits a unique personality. Let's examine them.

Needy Nelly

Nothing drives this particular single mom more than finding a husband to fix her loneliness. It makes perfect sense. If you want someone to conquer your lonesome nights, provide a second income for the family, and help raise the children, then you need a husband, right? Though that way of thinking is wrong, it is the mindset of millions of single moms. It was initially mine, but I didn't know any better.

The desire for a complete family unit remains bigger than life, and one goes to extremes to secure that. As for me, I actually considered forcing myself to fall in love with a chicken farmer. Now, don't get me wrong. I love chickens and farmers, but I am a city girl, not a country girl nor a chicken-farmer-type wife. In my desperation, I thought I could love this man. He would sweep me away into la-la land. I could be a Mrs. again. But there was one problem. When I took my children through his football-field-sized chicken houses, Jason and Sara hated the chickens: their smell, feathers, and clucks. My newfound "husband-to-be" did not appreciate the fact that my kids despised his chickens. My sister yanked me aside and scolded, "Pam, good grief. You're desperate. He's not for you." I had only known him for a few weeks, but what was the big deal?

Desperation during loneliness reminds us that only God can meet the deepest cravings of our soul. God made it that way by placing a vacuum in every heart that only He can fill. When a single mom rushes into the fantasy world of "this is the guy," she sets herself up for failure by inserting that man in God's vacuum. Statistics show that 67 percent of second marriages and 73 percent of third marriages end in divorce.[2] Why is that? Most single parents don't understand the concept of rebound, nor do they discover what needs to be healed in themselves before they pursue another relationship.

I asked Brad Goad, the singles' pastor at Second Baptist Church in Houston, who has been in ministry since the 1990s, "How long should a mom wait before dating again?" His answer did not surprise me. "It takes three to five years to walk through the process of healing." Another expert commented, "For every four years of marriage, it requires one year of healing." Friend, seeking a husband too soon can be disastrous, especially for the children. Here is my rule: if you are needy for a husband, you are not ready.

Be honest with yourself. Are you dating this person because you hope he will fill the void? Or are you seeing someone after the three- to five-year period, so that you have had time for God to heal the sore places? Dearest friend, be ever so cautious. I personally advise this, though I know it is not what you want to hear: stay single until the children graduate from high school. They will be under your roof for only a short time. They deserve your utmost attention while you have them in your care. Though I didn't do that myself, looking back, I see the wisdom in it. I have been married to Rich since the 1990s. He is an awesome, godly man—indeed, the best husband ever. However, some of our children carried their unresolved pain and emotions into their teenage years. The initial stages of blending a family are difficult on everyone. It's like two different families living under the same roof, with much stress on all sides.

However, the flip side of that statistic indicates that 27 to 33 percent of remarriages stay together. A relationship done God's way and in His timing remains a blessed union. God is good in working out early marriage struggles. Rich and I both attribute the success of our marriage to being committed and, more importantly, getting on our knees together in prayer at every junction of difficulty. My point is: be careful and prayerful. If you *need* a husband, you are not ready. In the meantime, take heart. Healthy children can and do emerge out of single-parent homes.

Jealous Jenny

Who, me, jealous? Perhaps you have suffered through occasional pity parties where jealousy is the keynote speaker. One of the hardest parts of being a single parent is seeing what everyone else possesses and desiring it for yourself. Jealousy is being a bit agitated with God that He did not give *you* those ornaments of joy.

I remember when I would pick up my children from Paula's, the babysitter. It would pain my soul if I arrived at five o'clock, which was when Paula's husband came home. Melissa, Sara's playmate, would run into her daddy's arms, but there would be no daddy's arms when we walked into our house. Was that jealousy? If that is the case, then every single mom suffers from its venom. Whether you are single by choice or because of someone else's decision, it takes a chunk out of your heart to know that you don't have what a husband can provide: intimate companionship, a second paycheck, a partner in the church service, and someone to ask about your day every evening.

Melissa, a single mom from Norman, Oklahoma, understands this problem.

I was convinced my husband was having an affair. I'd occasionally find bras and other women's clothing around the house that weren't mine. Finally the truth surfaced. He wasn't "seeing" another woman. He was "being" the woman. He was a cross dresser. After the divorce my son attended years of counseling. Was I jealous? Absolutely! I wanted what my spouse promised. I desired someone to talk to about our son's struggles. I longed for my friends' marriages, with enough money that I didn't have to worry about buying a saxophone for my child in band. It's a lonely existence when you yearn for what you don't have.

Jealousy surfaces as a dangerous byproduct of loneliness, and, left unattended, it can make our hearts and homes dismal. The greatest asset we have is God's affection. In Exodus 20:5, God informs the children of Israel, who were bowing down to false statues, *"For I am the Lord your God, a jealous God."* What does that mean? Friend, God is jealous when we give something that rightly belongs to Him to someone or something else. God wants to meet our needs with what a husband should provide. In Isaiah 54:5, He declares, *"For I am your Maker, your husband."*

Friend, fixating on what we don't have steals our worship and service from God. He knows what is in His storehouse, and He longs to give it to us, generously and abundantly. No wonder God is jealous when we settle for the cheaper trinkets of this world.

Temptation Tammy

Is the temptation to engage in premarital sex wrong? Temptation is never wrong. The enemy persistently places lures in the forefronts of our minds. That is his job, and he does it quite well. It's what we do with those enticements that determine if we have sinned against another, our own bodies, or even God.

Moms, let's be honest. The majority of you have enjoyed sex, but even though *he* is gone, the desire hasn't gone away. What is one to do? It doesn't help that loneliness hovers like a shadow at nightfall, serving as an invitation for sin. I understand. It's not so much that you yearn for the act of sex itself; rather, you long to feel desirable. It's a struggle—a *big* one! All a man has to do is give you a big ol' hug and you are a blob of silly putty in his hands.

However, the good part stops there. The ruinous consequences of engaging in premarital sex abound.

- In sexual sin we violate the sacredness of our own bodies, which were made for God-given and God-modeled love. In 1 Corinthians 6:18-29, our Creator describes our bodies as a sacred Holy Place.
- No other sin remains more damaging to our well-being than sexual sin (1 Corinthians 6:18). When we participate in intercourse, we create a soul tie with that person that entraps. When we collect soul tie after soul tie, we lose ourselves in self-induced grief and turmoil.
- Sexually transmitted diseases serve as one of the most prevalent predators of our culture. Half of all Americans contract an STD at some point in their lives.[3]
- An unwanted pregnancy, the strain of guilt, and the byproducts of shame leave grooves of regret in a soul.

Shamra, an unwed mom with two boys, shares:

Because of my cravings for male validation, I compromised my values doing what he wanted me to do, becoming who he wanted me to be. Somewhere in the murky process, I lost knowing me, just for that one moment of pleasure. Afterwards, I suffered with remorse, only to turn around and face the same dilemma again. Sex without Christ's love makes one even lonelier. My accountability partner has helped me tame this monster. I'm learning that Christ's presence fills those hunger pains for intimacy and can restore a pure and wholesome heart.

Sex without Christ's love makes one even lonelier.

Friend, the aspiration for intimacy with a mate won't go away any time soon, and neither will your enemy. He knows your vulnerable spots, but God knows them, too. That is why memorizing specific

Scriptures that pertain to your weaknesses serves as a powerful weapon against temptation. God's Word always contains the solution. 1 Corinthians 10:13 says, *"No temptation has overtaken you that is not common to man. God is faithful, and He will not let you be tempted beyond your ability, but with the temptation He will also provide a way of escape, that you might be able to endure it."*

Three weapons of truth prevail in this promise.

1. God remains true to His Word. We may not always be faithful in how we handle temptations, but God remains faithful always.

2. God will never allow us to be tempted above our level of spiritual maturity. We stand bigger than our enticements to sin.

3. God will provide a special means of escape. The way out always accompanies the temptation. It is our job to look for it.

Loneliness is a state of mind that builds destructive walls. God's loving heart builds a bridge of intimacy that alleviates emotional abandonment as a remedy for the orphaned soul. And what is God's comfort and cure for this destructive emotion?

PRACTICING GOD'S PRESENCE

I will not leave you comfortless. I will come to you.
John 14:18

Phenomena intrigue me. *Webster's Unabridged Dictionary* defines them as something extraordinary, exceptional, a wonder.[4] I love *The Twilight Zone*, a television thriller where each episode ends with an unforeseen twist. A few years ago, I pampered myself with a weekend extravaganza of reruns, viewing over fifteen shows. Can you imagine partaking in such an indulgence, frozen in front of the TV for two entire days with chips and salsa in hand? I never do that, but I loved it. Maybe that is another reason why I adore God's Word. The most stunning stories of incomparable marvels remain tucked inside the pages of the Bible, waiting for someone to step into the domain of the invisible genius of God.

Earth's Forty-Day Twilight Zone

One of my favorite seasons of unexpected happenings in Scripture is that of the death, burial, and resurrection of Christ before His ascension into Heaven. Jesus traveled the world wrapped in the mystery of His physical, resurrected body for forty days, appearing unannounced to many. During this time, God's glory gave mankind one last glimpse of the kingdom of Heaven. Can you imagine witnessing Christ's death and then seeing Him in your midst? When I get to Heaven, I want to talk to Cleopas about such an encounter. He and his friend enjoyed the company of a newfound friend without knowing it was Jesus. When God opened their eyes, they recognized the risen Messiah. Luke 24:31 reports, *"Then He vanished from their sight."*

Another twilight moment occurred with the disciples and Thomas. John 20:26 testifies, *"And then Jesus came into the room, the doors having been locked, and He stood in their midst saying, 'Peace be with you.'"* Did Jesus walk through the walls? Or did He— pow—just appear? Friend, whatever happened, I imagine that the disciples needed God's peace at that moment! Amen? All these episodes and more give me Holy Ghost goose bumps.

However, the most endearing occurrence revolves around Jesus instructing His eleven disciples to flee to Galilee and wait for Him. Imagine being those men. *"What's Jesus going to tell us? And will He pass through a rock to get here?"*

Behold—Jesus' Promise

In this next encounter, Jesus' love swells for single mothers in future generations. In *this* encounter, Jesus intends for every secluded soul to find comfort in His watchful care. In *this* encounter, He announces His greatest gift to you concerning your plight of raising children alone. In John 28:20, Jesus pledges, *"And lo (behold, surely), I am with you always, even to the end of the age."*

How often is *always?* The Greek translation implies a continual care that extends for all seasons, encompassing every hour of your day. *Always* means *always.*[6] In other words:

- Never will you find yourself forsaken by God because of an abortion, crime, or unplanned pregnancy.
- Never will you find yourself isolated from the Spirit because of insecurity over appearance or worth.

- Never will you find yourself forgotten by the Father because of an illness that took a loved one.

Loneliness does not mean that God is not there. Jesus steps into your famine of intimacy and comfort. In Hebrews 13:5, He says, *"Beloved, I will not in any way fail you nor give you up nor leave you without support. I will not, I will not, I will not in any degree leave you helpless nor let you down nor relax my hold on you."*

Friend, never will we escape the Father's notice. In Psalm 139:7-10, David contemplates that very thought:

Where can I go from your Spirit [power]? Or where can I flee from your presence [face]? If I ascend to heaven [scale the heights of knowledge], you are there. If I make my bed in the Sheol [live a life of hell on earth], you are there. If I take the wings of the dawn [fly to where the sun rises] or dwell in the remotest part of the sea [sink to the ocean floor], even there the strength of your hand will hold me.

Friend, I don't know where you land in the dimension of those possibilities, but God knows, and you are *not* without an invitation to experience the *twilight* of His presence.

What Is God's Presence?

After Jesus' ascension, God sent the Holy Spirit to dwell in every follower of Christ, enabling them to connect with the Father's assistance and wisdom. God makes Himself known when we surrender our lives to Jesus. The more we seek Him, the more attuned we become to His inner voice and the prompting of His Spirit. It is real. It is alive. It is wonderful.

However, knowing about His presence within us is not enough to counteract loneliness. The perfection of any skill requires repetition. Attuning to His inner radar system requires training our souls, inviting Christ into every moment, remaining cognizant that He is in our midst (Emmanuel, God with us), and imagining what His physical presence might look and feel like. Friend, what would happen if you recognized God's companionship at the dinner table by adding a chair? What if you buckled a seatbelt for

Jesus in your car as a reminder of His occupancy? What would happen to your children's spirits if they began anticipating His closeness? In time they would recognize heavenly whisperings in their hearts. Jesus' Spirit is in us, with us, always. He is here! He is at work. He is not obscure.

Something happens in our loneliness when we rehearse God's company. When the Almighty's breath invades our darkness, our "night"—whatever difficulty that might entail–becomes as bright as day. Why? Because God is *light*. Bringing thoughts of the Father's goodness and power into a downtrodden state of mind dispels its gloom. How can we activate this *light?* How can we put this truth into practice in our daily routines?

The *ABCs* of Overcoming Loneliness

Loneliness comes to each of us at one time or another. We can, however, find our way through its wilderness by following the simple alphabet of God's plan. Three steps work in setting us free: thinking, sinking, and linking.

A = Activate Right Thinking

Change starts in the mind. In order to turn *to* God, we must turn *away* from ourselves. Shellie, a mom with three children under seven, understands this principle:

> *My husband and I divorced because of his addiction to alcohol. It left me with a nagging sense of emptiness and restlessness over how I'm going to pay the bills. I struggle with loneliness, sometimes crying myself to sleep. By accepting this season and offering it up to God as an act of worship, I'm gaining headway in seeing Christ as my sole provider. I'm learning if I want a better tomorrow, I must invite Jesus into my tears. He's teaching me that if I can't trust Him "here," I can't trust Him anywhere.*

Friend, if we desire to know God's warmth, then we cannot continue living life the same way and expect new results. Right thinking fosters a right relationship with God. Do you want the assurance that God is active in your:

- parenting worries?
- legal issues?
- dreams and plans for the future?
- newfound illness?
- never-ending fight to survive?
- financial struggles?

The Bible declares in James 4:8, *"Draw near to God and He will draw near to you."* It is more than merely coming closer. It is relying on Christ and clinging to Him wholeheartedly. In return, God promises to come alongside, shoulder to shoulder, heart to heart.

One of the ways I trained my mind was a hobby that became my best friend: journaling. Women are feelers. When we write our thoughts on paper, unresolved rollercoaster emotions find release, and a channel of communing with God opens. For example, when you are reading the Bible, if a word or phrase jumps off the page and quickens your spirit, know that the Holy Spirit is talking to you. Meditate on the words. Write them down. It soothes the wound of loneliness and brings the darkness of emotional emptiness into the light.

I recall my journal writings on New Year's Eve when I was a single mom. I felt especially lonely on that holiday every year. Journaling became my date with God, where we would throw our own party. In time, my entries became less negative and more hopeful. Notice the progression of thoughts from year to year, all taken from my journals:

- *Lord, well, here it is again. Another year gone by. I'm still angry. It's not fair.*
- *Hi, Lord, looks like I'm starting the New Year with just You and me again. And by the way, will You bring me a mate this time next year?*
- *Happy New Year, God. I'm so glad we can share these 365 days together. I can't wait to see what You'll do with them.*

Friend, I still have an appointment with God every New Year's Eve. Looking back, I see how my depression wooed me to Him for a lifetime. Our loneliness cannot always be fixed, but it can be accepted as God's will at the time. There is purpose in what feels like misfortune.

Think well, and remember that God makes everything beautiful in His time.

B = Be Still

The most severe form of loneliness stems from estrangement from God. When you fill your God-vacuum with anything or anyone other than Jesus, emotional imbalance ensues. No one understands the complexities of our loneliness more than our Creator does. Some single moms forget that truth. Instead of running to Jesus first, they seek the comfort of a coworker or male friend. God knows more than anyone how to soothe our sorrows. The remedy comes by practicing silence and solitude.

- In Matthew 11:28, Jesus beckons, *"Come to Me, all who are weary and heavy laden, and I will give you rest."*
- In Psalm 46:10, God instructs David, *"Cease striving and know that I am God."*
- In Jeremiah 20:13, it is declared, *"God has delivered the life of the needy; sing to the Lord."*

Coming grants *knowing,* and *knowing* grants *singing.* Come. Know. Sing. But what happens when we get those out of order? Or what if we are too busy to come? It leaves us imprisoned in our loneliness. Only Jesus can break those chains of confinement, bringing the solace of His perspective into the prison cell.

Friend, what if I told you that participating in an activity fifteen minutes a day would grant contentment? Would you get up earlier in the morning, or sit under a shady tree at lunch to find it? What is God's wisdom, refreshment, and joy worth to you?

Vikki, a widow from Kentucky with two girls, explores that thought.

My husband was murdered in our home while my children slept in the next room. I was away on a business trip. Some days its horror haunts me where it hurts too much to even breathe. But when I open God's Word, a peace I cannot explain comes over me that calms this hellish nightmare. I actually feel God's presence descend, lift my anguish, and physically hold me tight. His words swell off those pages giving me comfort like none other. It helps me seeing how God enabled biblical characters just like me in getting through the worst tragedies imaginable. God's Word is alive, alive, alive because its author is alive.

Friend, it is impossible to find peace of mind and genuine hope if you allow God's love letter, the Bible, to sit on the shelf collecting dust. Its words are not just *words*. They are sparks from the throne of the Almighty, ushering His provisions to your cause, transforming your ability to cope. Dr. Tallie, an expert in counseling single parents, affirms, "God's Word gives single mothers the power to overcome emotional energy that's being drained out of them while giving outside energy to draw from."

Friend, what do you need at this moment: emotional ease, divine insight, gutsy courage, infinite confidence? Nothing matters more than seeing Jesus' arms extended to you from those pages in Scripture. Following a car accident, one goes to the hospital for one's physical wounds. But where does one go after an emotional crash? Go to God's Word. It miraculously heals wounds and repairs feelings. Dwight L. Moody expressed it well when he said, "The Bible was not intended to increase your knowledge but to *change your life.*"

Halt your hectic schedule and bring God into the moment. You are never less alone than when you spend time alone with God. Allow His Word to "sink well" into your greatest concern. It is solitary *refinement* at its best.

You are never less alone than when you spend time alone with God.

C = Connect

For many single moms, the word *connect* strikes a bad chord. It pushes them out of their comfort zone of isolation. One single mom testified, "I've tried to bond with others. I'd rather stay lonely than take the risk of letting someone discover the hidden me."

There is only one, big problem with that. It is not God's plan. You need others and others need you. Your children will one day graduate, the house will creak with stillness, and then what will you do? Liberate yourself from lingering loneliness by sharing your life with others. Dr. Les Carter calls it *linking well*. What does it look like to *link well*?

Healing from loneliness happens one layer at a time. Emotional wellness stems from healthy friendships. They give you a sense of belonging and acceptance. Often, after a divorce or other form of rejection, you wonder if you have anything to offer. Many misunderstand the term *togetherness*, thinking it relates only to male-female relationships. But healthy *togetherness* finds its strength in same-sex friendships. Though male friends can serve a unique purpose, many women don't realize their own vulnerability. Male friendships often turn into a romantic relationship too soon. When that happens, the mom thinks she is *healing*. She is not. She is seeing a mirage that does nothing more than distract her from her unresolved emotions.

Another crucial factor in linking well is finding a church home. I have heard moms say they have visited churches and felt like outcasts. Try another one and another one until you locate a body of believers that teaches the Word of God and embraces your family as a precious addition to their fellowship. You have much to give to a group. Find one.

Rebekah, a single mom from Oklahoma City with two teenagers, expressed:

My church is our second family. It's our social life. We're learning to pray as a family. My children love the Bible truths and they're finding male role models. And I love my small group, a safe place where we share our weaknesses, needs, and joys. We love each other in Christ. I'm celebrating my singleness.

Locating a church family remains *the most* valuable asset to you and your children.

Giving

In life, there are givers and takers. Most single moms begin as takers, and that's good if you have others to help you. However, a time comes when it is healthy to pull alongside others. God's Word promises a unique blessing to those who refresh others. Your peers need to know that you have experienced the same complications they have and survived. It boosts their faith and reinforces yours. It is what you sow that multiplies, not what you keep in the barn.

Find ways to serve in the community. Volunteer for a charity with your children. Invite your support group to the park. Ask God where to join with others and how to fulfill His Word among them.

- Encourage one another—Hebrews 3:13
- Admonish one another—Colossians 3:16
- Accept one another—Romans 14: 1
- Build up one another—1 Thessalonians 5:11
- Be hospitable to one another—1 Peter 4:9

God blesses you to make you a blessing to others. You make a difference, so *link well*. A life worth living gives itself away.

Loneliness, like a coin, has two sides. On one face, it is painful suffering in a deserted wilderness, a problem that you never wanted, resulting in a life of self-centeredness. On the flip side, it is a burst of God's presence through the lens of grace, something you have always wanted, resulting in a life of holiness. The coin is in your hand. You determine on which side it lands.

Whispers from Jesus

I am with you. You will never face an issue with your children or personal life without My presence. You want to get out of your loneliness, but I am allowing you to stay in it. I am training you to know the reality of My nearness. It is in the dark of life that you more easily hear My voice. Sit still in My light. I will not leave you as an orphan. I will come to you. When you are lonely, hear My whisper, "I cherish you, My love."

Silent Reflection

1. Which best describes you: Needy Nelly, Jealous Jenny, or Temptation Tammy?

2. How does Jesus' "Behold Promise" comfort you?
3. In what way does Romans 8:35-37 relate to you?
4. In the *ABCs* of overcoming loneliness, which step did you find the hardest to do?
5. Jesus was a single adult. How did He handle His loneliness?

Gentle Respite for the Soul

God Upholds

2 Timothy 4:16-17—*All deserted me, but the Lord stood with me and strengthened me.*

Psalm 46:1—*God is our refuge and strength, a very present help in times of trouble.*

God Tends

Psalm 4:8—*The Lord cares for us and makes a home for the lonely.*

Psalm 147:3—*He heals the brokenhearted and binds up their wounds. He counts the number of the stars; He gives names to all of them. Great is our Lord, and abundant in strength; His understanding is infinite.*

God Abides

Exodus 34:4—*My presence shall go with you and I will give you rest.*

Psalm 42:5—*Praise Him for the help of His presence.*

CHAPTER SIX

From the Falsehood of Low Self-Worth to Knowing Your Identity in Christ

Our adequacy comes from God.
2 Corinthians 3:5b

For two days I sat, stumped, at my computer. I didn't know what to name this chapter. With volumes written on how a woman seeks her identity through the sieve of this world rather than through the eyes of God's grace through Christ, I pondered which title best fit the single mom's journey to find her true self. If you don't like my title, pick another that describes your hidden wound, the one that only you and God have eyes to see. Alternatives include:

- From the Falsehood of Marred Integrity to Knowing Your Identity in Christ
- From the Falsehood of Deflated Self-Importance to Knowing Your Identity in Christ
- From the Falsehood of Repulsed Self-Disgust to Knowing Your Identity in Christ

These hurt, much like washing down a giant pill of insecurity with the juice of lowliness. Whichever one defines your rollercoaster ride, the solution remains clear. You must "nail down" on the track *this* rail of truth: it is not *self*-esteem you need, but *God*-esteem.

Esteem Machine

To "esteem" means to set a high value on something. "Self-esteem" means to have a positive regard for oneself. It exposes the degree to which one feels valued and acknowledged. In biblical times, gold and other precious metals were placed on a scale and their worth was determined by their weight. Our first perception of our "weight of worth" is based on the scales of our parents' hands. In later years, other influences mold how we feel about ourselves: peers, experiences, marital status, and more.

The source of our self-esteem resembles a rocket booster that propels a spacecraft in its journey. I am not an electrical engineer nor did I receive a call yesterday from NASA concerning their aeronautics research, but I do have an elementary understanding of the purpose of the booster. Many remember the space shuttle *Challenger,* which malfunctioned seventy-three seconds after liftoff, killing seven astronauts. A faulty fuel rocket promises disaster.

I know single moms who wonder why their shuttles of worth are not gaining altitude above their losses and feelings of shame. Every attempt to project upward into the realm of positive identity ends with a splashdown only seventy-three seconds after blastoff. What is the problem? It's certainly not because God's plan for your emotional and spiritual wholeness powered down. Why do moms feel trapped in low self-regard, suffocating in the fumes of inferiority?

Defective Rocket Boosters

Answer these questions:

- What or who defines your identity?
- Where do you turn to find meaning in life?
- What makes you feel significant?

Your answers serve as rocket-booster indicators. You are either being pulled upward by a Christ-centered focus or being held back by a world-centered focus. When we received Christ, we were not only empowered to view ourselves from His perspective, but His Holy Spirit entered our "spacecraft" for the duration of the flight. In Christ we find our true significance. However, many discover their importance other places. In the Bible, King Saul felt his value through power. Ananais and Sapphira based their worth on money. The Galatians established their righteousness on circumcision. Saul (before he became Paul) believed that his religious pedigree gave him worth. Where do you find your deepest sense of value?

A Boyfriend

Society teaches that if you don't have a mate, something is wrong with you. Add that to your *husbandless* family unit, and you can see why single moms feel incomplete in both their household structure and personal identity. While engaging in a male relationship might feel wonderful at first, it is a flawed source of worth. Joy and stability—the fuel for your personal "happiness tank"—do not come from another human being. Moms who carry that mindset find themselves deflated when their new mates don't meet their expectations. Wholeness does not come from marriage. It comes from the Holy Spirit esteeming Himself *in* and *through* you.

The Children

It is normal to find your identity in your kids. The only problem is, what if they disappoint you? What if you raise them properly, but they spiritually rebel? You feel like a failure, exposed as a bad mother. You deem yourself responsible to fix it, but you feel defensive and trapped. Even if the children do turn out well, becoming a pastor, schoolteacher, or company CEO, you still can't take total credit. It is by the grace of God that any of our children turn out well. Friend, one day you will face an empty nest. Nothing is more deflating than waving goodbye to your son or daughter, then looking in the mirror with bewilderment and asking, *"Who are you?"* Becky, a single mom from Illinois, relates:

I've been a single mom for twenty-three years. My son's graduating in May. When he leaves, what will my core identity be then? I've lost myself in the journey.

A Dangerous Place

After my husband left I gazed in the mirror and thought, *What's wrong with me? I'm precious.* Though I didn't feel unworthy, I did become a gym rat for a short period. Maybe I was releasing stress and energizing myself to raise Jason and Sara alone. Maybe I needed a reprieve from the living room cluttered with toys. Good cover, Pam. No, the truth is that I wanted somebody in that place to think I was desirable. It was a daunting experience the first time I walked into that facility without my wedding ring. I froze in disbelief when I realized that men were thinking the same thing I was. I had never considered that my ring conveyed an unspoken message: *I'm taken.* With it off my finger, the world became a dangerous place. So what did I do? I grabbed my children from the daycare and ran home like Little Red Riding Hood.

What defines your value? Is it your possessions, career status, personal giftedness, volunteer work, church activities, or friendships? What happens when a woman's worth is found in anything other than in what God says? She falls prey to a host of unpleasant consequences that counterfeit her highest God-ordained calling.

Dr. Hat Maker

Nobody likes to be the object of fury, hatred, and destruction, but as Christ's followers, we are that target. In 1 Peter 5:8, it says, *"Your adversary the devil is a roaring lion [in fierce hunger] seeking someone to devour"* (swallow down). When we surrendered our lives to Jesus, we became a new creation, adorned on the inside with Christ's beauty, which defines the essence of our esteem. But the devil doesn't want us to know the good news. He is bent on seeing us minimized, demoralized, or scrutinized. He paces back and forth and strategizes. The devil is on a mission. Having acquired a Ph.D. with his dissertation, "How to Deceive Single Moms into Wearing Hats," he expedites his shrewd plot by displaying his latest collection: hats that distort our perception of identity, speak falsehoods about our value, and make us feel insignificant and defeated. Unaware of his strategy, we wear them proudly.

Hat Parade

If we don't cover our heads with God's truth, Satan covers them with his lies. As you fight to keep your head above water, the enemy reaches to pull you under. How does he do that? He calculates which hat design best fits your weaknesses and struggles. Notice the cunning creativity of his four types of hats and how each one festers untruths about your worth.

If we don't cover our heads with God's truth, Satan covers them with his lies.

The Baseball Cap

This hat is the most common in the enemy's assortment. It keeps the "Sonshine" out of one's eyes, blocking the rays of spiritual truth. While visors are supposed to protect our eyes from harmful rays, this one prevents us from seeing our value as children of God. Its embroidered inscription fits well on the front center: *I am inadequate.*

Marilyn, a single mother with two boys, shares:

I come from a family of strong women. Women who cook, clean, have their makeup on perfectly, hair combed. Women who are at every church function. Some days I'm lucky to just get my teeth brushed. I compare myself and end up on the losing end. I lose my keys, credit cards, and my temper on a regular basis. I'm late to everything and my house is a mess. I'm a single mother by choice, and obviously a poor one at that.

Marlene, a single mother with a boy and two girls, comments:

A friend of mine asked if I'd take her thirteen-month-old grandson for an indefinite period of time. She abandoned him and the baby's mother passed away. I'm raising this boy, and I'm falling apart. I'm a hundred pounds overweight. I'm crying out to God. I'm so ill equipped to do this.

My former husband's grandmother told me before he remarried, "Pam, my grandson told me today that I'd really adore his new wife. He said she's a lot like you." I thought, *Then why did he leave "me" for another "me"?*

The Bucket Hat

Gilligan from *Gilligan's Island* models this hat well. With a downward-sloping brim, it causes one to vanish in a crowd. It enhances the false belief that there is something wrong with who you are. Tucked in its inner lining lurks the secret message: *I am defective.*

Carol, a single mother with two girls, confesses:

I've lived with depression and suicidal thoughts for twenty-five years. I will never be good enough, never be worthy of love, and never find peace. I was raped twice while in high school, believing I'm dirty in the eyes of God. How could a holy God look at such filth? How could He love someone like me, marred by something so reprehensible and degrading?

Sherry, a single mom with two teenagers and a grandson, recounts:

I'm thirty-eight years old. My son's dad walked out when I was pregnant. For over ten years I've lived with the guilt and disgrace believing no one would ever want me and my baggage.

Valinda, a single mom with two girls, admits:

I'm ashamed. I've had an abortion. Every time I see a pregnant woman, I'm reminded of how I killed my child. Why did I listen to my boyfriend, who's now in prison? Noises haunt me, like the vacuum cleaner, a reminder of what took place in that clinic. I'm less than a person, half of a mother.

The Trapper Hat

This style offers protection from the elements. It provides warmth with a fur interior, but earflaps keep us wrapped up in the belief that we did something wrong. Somehow we have the misconception that we are to blame for our predicament; therefore, *I am a failure.*

Chiquita, a single mother with one boy and two girls, recalls:

Because I wasn't able to keep my marriage together, I resembled a flop. *My former spouse and I were both in full-time ministry with him being a pastor. I failed God. I failed the church. I failed my children.*

Paula, a single mom with a boy and a girl expresses:

I've always been respected, a leader, a godly example, popular. Never has there been a divorce in my family line. I hate being a scarred woman.

Shan, a single mother with two boys and a girl, discloses:

I'm trapped in a lifestyle I can't get out of: drugs, miscarriages, physical abuse. The state agency took my son and entrusted him to my parents. I can't do anything right.

The Beanie Cap

This knit cap remains Satan's favorite style, one that fits tightly around the head and constricts correct thinking. Life as a single mother can push you to the edge, no longer willing to persevere through the hard times. This cap's message: *I am giving up.*

Holly, a single mother of one son, confides:

While growing up, my mom took my younger brother and me to church. I always thought those "church people" had attained some higher calling. Over time I grew into an approval addict in order to feel like I mattered. I hoped I'd please my supervisor, my parents. I devalued myself by giving men whatever they needed: money, possessions, sex. After marrying my husband, the marriage began to unravel where even motherhood didn't fill those hollow spots.

After my husband held me down on the couch with my arms extended backwards, I called the police, grabbed my son, and fled to a homeless shelter. A nasty custody battle ensued. I won the court case, but my affinity for male validation continued. My counselor pinpointed the problem: I was a sex addict, which came from a depressive disorder. That announcement pushed me over the top. My son deserved a better mom—a whole and complete one—a mother who's not so broken. I had two options: give him up for adoption or kill myself.

A sense of inferiority is the genesis of low self-worth and the hat maker's number-one psychological weapon. I am disheartened after reading these stories, along with hundreds of others that I have collected. They echo a common message about one's value: *I am trapped in a bottomless cavity of hopelessness, and I cannot get out.*

Friend, yes you can! No matter how far you have fallen, you will never descend beyond God's grace. Because of Christ, you are worthy of self-respect. It's time to break through Satan's pack of lies and reclaim what has been lost: your self-esteem. Why model Satan's hats when God has given you a crown?

No matter how far you have fallen, you will never descend beyond God's grace.

KNOWING YOUR IDENTITY IN CHRIST

For I [my self-esteem] have been crucified with Christ. It is no longer I who lives but Christ [God-esteem] who lives in me.
Galatians 2:20

I asked more than two hundred women in a seminar, "What does it mean to have an identity in Christ?" The response surprised me. Few knew how to define it, while the majority didn't understand how *identity* related to *Christ*. Satan writes on the chalkboard of our minds, reminding us of all the ways we fall short. Somewhere along the way, Christian leaders and parents have failed to teach us about our immense wealth in God.

Never has there been a topic more imperative and less talked about than knowing who we are in Christ. Seeing ourselves through God's lens is paramount.

- It's the key to breaking away from patterns of feeling shame, trying harder, and quitting.
- It's the way to experience God's supernatural power in living beyond ourselves.
- It's the foundation to claiming a reality that empowers personal change.

Knowing our identity in Christ releases us from life's gravity.

No Longer a Clean Clunker

We all get our identity from somewhere. *Webster's* defines *identity* as an "exact likeness in nature or qualities."[1] For example, as a teenager, I based my identity on my friends. The quality of my friendships defined my wellbeing. What does it mean to base our qualities on someone else's nature—our character traits, instincts, and disposition?

When I surrendered my life to Christ at eight years old, a divine transformation took place in my soul. I inherited Christ's nature. My old practices subsided. New patterns and principles came to life. The self-dominated me moved out. The Jesus-dominated me moved in.

This experience of yielding control over my life to Jesus (called salvation or conversion) reminds me of a red jalopy that belonged to my boyfriend in high school. Whenever he took it through the car wash, it came out a clean clunker. But what would happen if, right between the soapy suds and final rinse, a firsthand engine were dropped under the hood? It would no longer be a shiny clunker but a brand-new model.[2] That is what happens when we give our lives to Christ. We receive an inside makeover, becoming someone we have never been before. Because of God's grace and Christ's sacrifice on the cross, we are declared new creations. We are no longer clunkers but original Ferraris, able, through the power of the Holy Spirit, to redirect unhealthy emotions, recharge fatigue, and navigate life with precision. We acquire a new bodysuit, one complete with divine resources that enable godly living and insight.

Friend, we have what is needed to overcome low self-esteem. The *good* that God wants to channel through our lives trumps embedded negative thoughts about our value. God's truth has been placed within us, waiting for release. We have blessings. We have benefits. And although we still struggle with the flesh and other competing passions, underneath our dysfunctional pasts and current insecurities resides a radical new nature, implanted and sustained by God Himself. Our greatest dilemma as single moms becomes *not* how we can "fix" ourselves but how we can "release" our new natures.[3]

The Real Me

When is the last time you considered the wonder of you? You have been granted so much God-favor that if you could see your potential, you wouldn't recognize yourself. You are not who you think you are. You are much, much more. However, therein lies the problem. Most single moms don't live out their amazing potential.

You are not who you think you are. You are much, much more.

Second Corinthians 5:17 declares, *"If any man be in Christ, he is a new creation, old things have passed away; behold, all things have become new."* The Greek word for *new creation* means not only have I received a new kind of *being,* but also I have received a new kind of *situation* in which to handle my *being.*[4] In other words, we are not confined to our hurts, hangups, or habits. The Holy Spirit enables us to thrive in a *new situation*—a new domain—one that sanctions us to address our trials with a new set of principles and expectations. And although our old ways still linger, we have a new desire for the Spirit to override them. In Christ, we live out of God's anointment instead of our disappointment. Say goodbye to low-self esteem. God has created a new world in our souls.

In Christ, we live out of God's anointment
instead of our disappointment.

Are You Sitting Down?

That is a phrase someone uses when they have big news to share. Are you ready? The "real" you was born to be blessed. In my book and Bible study, *Will the Real Me Please Stand Up,* I listed 100 attributes that followers of Christ possess. They each define our spiritual blessings, and they all begin with the words, *I am.* They speak of who we are in Christ. What a thrill to contemplate the unfathomable riches we can claim as children of the King! Some of the blessings are:

- *I am* alive to God.
- *I am* an overcomer.
- *I am* content with difficulties.
- *I am* attended by angels.
- *I am* God's delight.

Two more speak of our immense value to God. I especially adore these two, which touch deeply in a single mother's heart: *I am loved by God*, and *I am complete in Christ*.

I Am Loved by God

Why do these words feel awkward, as if they aren't true for *you?* When we have been disappointed, abandoned, or abused, and especially if we didn't have a nurturing earthly father, it is easy to form an incorrect view of God: cold, distant, and ready to smack us with His discipline rod. However, nothing could be farther from the truth. God is love. Why can't we feel that reality? Often, we cannot understand the magnitude of God's love for us. However, we can understand our love for our own children. So consider this.

As a parent, how do you feel when your son walks into the room? Do you love him more if he enters with a smile on his face? Do you love him less if dirt is smudged across his brow? Whether he is all cleaned up or soiled from head to toe, it doesn't alter your love for him. He is your child, and you are his parent. He has been invited to call you "Mommy." Likewise, God is your Heavenly parent. You are His child. You have been invited to call Him "Abba," an Aramaic word that means *Daddy* or *Papa*. Papa God longs for this kind of personal closeness. His love for us far exceeds the love we possess for our own sons and daughters.

Matthew 7:11 says, *"If you, being evil, know how to give good gifts to your children, how much more shall your Father who is in heaven give what is good to those who ask Him!"* Notice the exclamation point. Rarely do you see that in Scripture. And notice the word *more*. God's generous heart resides far outside our human understanding.

Friend, you are loved! Whether or not you see it, feel it, or believe it doesn't change the truth of it. Never will there be a time in your "single-mom life" that your Eternal Daddy will abandon His love or ignore your call for help. When you are ready to give up, His Word has a response:

- *I can't live like this.* I will supply your needs (Philippians 4:19).
- *I am too tired.* I will give you rest (Matthew 11:28-30).
- *I am a failure.* I began a good work in you. I will complete it (Philippians 1:6).
- *I am tempted.* I will deliver you out of temptation (2 Peter 2:9).
- *I can't handle this.* You possess my risen power (2 Timothy 1:7).
- *Nobody loves me.* I love you (John 3:16).[5]

I often hear from single moms, "How could God love me? I've done so many horrible things. Guilt and shame keep me from God because I don't deserve His love." Friend, none of us deserves it.

Ephesians 2:8 says, *"For by grace you have been saved through faith, and that, not of yourself, it is a gift from God, not as a result of works, that no one should boast."* God's love is a gift. We didn't earn it; therefore, we cannot lose it. Nothing can separate us from His affection.

Romans 8:35-39 says:

Is anything able to drive a wedge between Christ's love and us? There is not. Not trouble, not hard times, not hatred, not hunger, not homelessness, not bullying threats, not backstabbing, not even the worst sins listed in Scripture. Nothing living or dead, angelic or demonic, today or tomorrow, high or low, thinkable or unthinkable—absolutely nothing can get between us and God's love because of the way that Jesus our Master has embraced us.

Not one thing can block God's love from us. What is your "one thing"? Is it regret, an addiction, sexual promiscuity, a prison sentence, an unbridled tongue? Our list grows by the minute. Our sins might cause us to temporarily lose fellowship with God until we turn back to Him, but He never stops loving us.

Friend, accept what the Father says about you.

- *You are beautiful and there is no blemish in you* (Song of Solomon 4:7).
- *Anyone who touches you touches the apple of My eye* (Zechariah 2:8).
- *I will establish with you an everlasting covenant* (Ezekiel 16:60).

Papa God is calling you at this moment to run into His arms. Will you?

Dear Heavenly Daddy, I have never felt that I deserve Your love. But because you cherish me, that alone makes me worthy to unwrap Your gift of grace and enjoy its benefits. Help me to experience unconditional adoration.

I Am Complete in Christ

Do you feel incomplete because you don't have a spouse? A household with children *should* have a mommy and daddy living under the roof, right? But yours does not. Those emotional rainclouds that hover above cause teardrops when you least expect it. For example, have you felt a sting when asked on an application form to answer the question: *married or single?* Why does it matter? It feels like a hidden message that says, *If you're not married, you're not complete.*

How does one overcome feeling like half of a person? It hurts, because you were designed to be connected to another. Our Creator knows that well. He has provided a higher plain of living, one that meets our longing for companionship. In the early church at Colossae, the false teachers taught that God's fullness came through philosophy and good works. Paul rebuked them, saying that any attempt to find completeness in anything other than Christ leads to empty deception. When we received Christ, we inherited unlimited access to all God owns.

What does incompleteness look like where you live? How

does it affect your needs as a single mom? In 2 Peter 1:3, God's Word proclaims, *"In Christ you have everything you need for life and godliness."* Though some traits may be undeveloped, you have what you need to grow in Christ and make it through any difficulty. Friend, you don't have to live in the gloom of aloneness, inadequacy, or deficiency. God has given you the resource of His catalogue of names. We have only one name, but God has many, each one articulating His attributes that both define who He is and support us when our faith tank is low. Are you calling on them? Do you know God's smorgasbord of names? They are potent allies in your march to victory.

- *El Shaddai:* "Almighty God," the One who supplies and comforts
- *Elohim:* "Strong One," the One who creates
- *El Roi:* "Seeing God," the One who watches
- *El Elyon:* "Most High God," the One who remains sovereign
- *El Olam:* "Everlasting God," the One who never changes
- *Emmanuel:* "God with Us," the One who never leaves our side
- *Jehovah Jireh:* "Lord of Provisions," the One who provides
- *Jehovah Raah:* "The Lord My Shepherd," the One who attends
- *Jehovah Nissi:* "The Lord My Banner," the One who fights
- *Jehovah Rapha:* "Healer," the One who restores
- *Jehovah Shalom:* "The Lord My Peace," the One who awards rest

Perhaps you need to call on one of those names right now:

- *El Roi, I'm a solo mother carrying the load. Help me remember that You keep an eye out for me.*
- *Jehovah Nissi, I'm a solo mother engaging in battle. Help me recall that You fight for me.*
- *Jehovah Raah, I'm a solo mother feeling lost as a sheep. Help me remember that You care for me.*

Remember the testimonies of single moms in the "hat parade"? By calling on God's names, they found an ally on their battlefields. Chiquita: *I love what Elohim, my Creator, is showing me. I'm fearfully and wonderfully made and there isn't anything that I can't do through Christ who gives me strength. So I'll plan, dream, invent, then focus and walk it out. My Father is for me. I'm God's girl. How can I be "without"?*

Marlene: *God gave me the thirteen-month-old boy for a reason. He knew the mother was going to die. Now he's my son, seven years old. Jehovah Jireh, my Provider, has overcome every crisis. I've lost my hundred pounds, come out of a depression. My church community is my support. God's filling never fails.*

Carol: *I've overcome my rape shame. I'm not disgusting or unworthy of God's love. I'm transformed by God's grace, mercy, and cleansing power. When He looks upon me, He sees my robe of righteousness. I am beautiful to Him. I've been restored to inner wholeness by Jehovah Rapha, my Healer.*

Holly: *I'm a great mom. I'm in this life for a purpose. No longer do I find my value in men. I'm abstinent by choice and Christ is meeting that emptiness. I'm getting to know the "real" me, a lovely creation. God's revealing Himself as El Shaddai, the All-Sufficient God. I have unlimited access to whatever I need. My life story has just begun.*

In Christ, there is no shortage. In Christ is fullness of joy. Your home is not incomplete. God is the *"Father to the Fatherless"* (Psalm 68:5), and *"the Lord your Maker is your husband"* (Psalm 54:5).

You are *complete* in Christ:

- *Fully* forgiven—Colossians 2:13
- *Fully* accepted and reconciled to God—2 Corinthians 5:18
- *Fully* adopted as an heir (not a stepchild)—Romans 8:15
- *Fully* indwelt by the Holy Spirit—1 Corinthians 3:16
- *Fully* holy and blameless—Ephesians 1:4
- *Fully* adequate—2 Corinthians 3:5b
- *Fully* comforted—2 Corinthians 1:4
- *Fully* favored—Ephesians 1:3
- *Fully* Heaven bound—John 3:16

Who are you in Christ? You are complete as *one* woman, *one* single mom. Do you feel like less than that? Do you feel as if you are half of a whole? How can that be? The number one is not a fraction but a "whole" number.

Whispers from Jesus

I see your inadequacy. I am the God of abundance and I will never run out of resources. Your name is inscribed on the palms of My hands. You are never out of My sight, never abandoned. Your deepest wants lead you to the discovery that I alone complete you. When you feel as though you have been cast aside, hear My whisper, "I cherish you, My love."

Silent Reflection

1. What determines your self-image?
2. Which one of Dr. Hat Maker's inventions best fits you? Explain.
3. Discuss the spiritual magnitude of 2 Corinthians 5:17.
4. Comment on each of the five *I am* blessings taken from *Will the Real Me Please Stand Up*.
5. How did you relate to each name of God?

Gentle Respite for the Soul

God Appoints Purpose

Matthew 5:13a, 15:16—*You are the salt of the earth. . . . Let your light shine before men in such a way that they may see your good works, and glorify your Father who is in Heaven.*

Ephesians 2:10—*We are His workmanship created in Christ Jesus to do good works, which God prepared beforehand, that we should walk in them.*

God Bestows Value

Isaiah 62:5b—*As a bridegroom rejoices over his bride, so will your God rejoice over you.*

Zephaniah 3:17—*The Lord your God is in your midst, a victorious warrior. He will exult over you with joy, He will be quiet in His love, He will rejoice over you with shouts of joy.*

God Instills Significance

Psalm 139:17-18—*How precious to me are Your thoughts, O God! How vast is the sum of them! Were I to count them, they would outnumber the grains of sand. When I awake, I am still with You.*

Isaiah 49:15-16—*Can a mother forget the baby at her breast and have no compassion on the child she has borne? Though she may forget, I will not forget you! See, I have engraved you on the palm of My hands; your walls are ever before Me.*

CHAPTER SEVEN

From the Swells of Guilt to Abounding in God's Grace

There is no condemnation for those in Christ.
Romans 8:1

I have never known a single mother who does not, at least to some degree, swim in the waters of guilt. While gasping for air—in need of a larger bank account, a clock with more hours, or a manual on either co-parenting or parenting alone—she paddles with all her might to stay afloat. I looked up *guilt* in *Webster's*. I was shocked. It didn't list the synonym *mother-like*. I am not sure there is a mama out there (single or otherwise) who hasn't felt the drowning swell of guilt at one time or another.

The Ugly Emotions

What are shame and guilt? While very much alike, they are distinctly different. Shame is tied to judgments about who we are in our personhood; guilt is tied to feelings about what we do in our behavior. Shame murmurs, *I am a mistake.* Guilt says, *I made a mistake.* However, in this chapter, their uniqueness doesn't matter. They are both dreadful emotions, two thieves crucifying us between regret of the past and fear of the future. With a nagging awareness of our shortcomings, they disable our ability to reason well and enjoy life. They minimize our esteem and energy while leading us into depression, comparisons, perfectionism, blame, and various addictions. And the worst part is that the victim often feels as if he or she is living a lie. Behind every friendly "hello" lurks a silent message that shrieks, *I'm tired of not being me (whoever that is)!* Shame and guilt left in the basement of our souls hamper the fullness of Christ-generated joy.

Top-Ten Countdown—Why I Feel Guilty as a Single Mom

The bond single moms share is astonishing. They belong to their own underground sorority, "The Single-Mom Sisterhood," with each member joined at the hip. They understand one another well. There is a saying: "misery loves company." For this group, I would rather say, "Trials bring co-hearts." Do any of these top-ten guilt inducers, listed from least potent to most poignant, ring a bell with you?

10. Hearing innocent comments such as: "Mommy, we just want you to play with us every once in a while."
9. Believing if you were a better mom the children wouldn't be in this predicament
8. Feeling that your family unit is not normal
7. Dating
6. Losing your temper or not being more emotionally stable
5. Having to be the good cop and the bad cop
4. Not attending your children's school plays, sports activities, and award banquets
3. Lacking money for fun stuff
2. Not having enough time for family
1. Fearing that your children are disadvantaged because there is no male role model in the home

If that is not enough, here is one single mom's take on it.

If I overreact in disciplining the children, I feel guilty. If I underreact by letting them get away with murder, I feel guilty.

If I overcompensate by buying goodies to fix their unhappiness, I feel guilty. If I undercompensate by not buying treats, I feel guilty.

If I over-evaluate that I work too much, I feel guilty. If I under-evaluate that I need to work more, I feel guilty.

If I over-dwell on my own childhood advantages (like vacations), I feel guilty. If I under-dwell that my kids have no advantages and never get out of town, I feel guilty.

At all times and in every way I feel overloaded, overtaxed, overstretched, and downright g-u-i-l-t-y!

Friend, if you have suffered from only one of these, that's huge;

however, many agonize over all of them simultaneously. The *would have, should have, could haves* along with the *oughts* and *nots* loom over your life. The symptoms of persistent shame and guilt camouflage themselves well, and they are all results of a shame-based identity. The moms suffering from them know that something is wrong; they just can't peg the inner perpetrator. The effects of this foul duo are just as diverse as the reasons behind them. What do the manifestations of these two soul slayers look like?

Swells of Shame: Her Voice Cries Out

I Am a Bad Person

The mom with this mindset carries her own brand of dishonor. Feeling inconsequential, she is not surprised that nothing ever works in her favor: the other woman gets the raise, her best friend gets engaged, the kids think their dad is more fun than she is. If someone compliments her, she feels awkward. Like oil dropped in a cup of water, it doesn't mix well with her personal value system. However, she does have one intimate friend: her inner voice, the one that converses with her conscience as faithfully as the earth rotates around the sun:

- *If you weren't socially awkward, you'd have more friends.*
- *No wonder nobody asks you out. Who wants to marry a woman fifty pounds overweight with three children and $7,000 in debt?*
- *If you had been a better sexual partner, he wouldn't have split the scene.*
- *How could you be so stupid to think your son would give you a birthday card?*
- *You deserve to be a widow.*

This single mom lives in a preoccupation of fault and blame that feeds her guilt. How can she make a paradigm shift from dysfunctional "self-talk" to edifying "God-talk"?

I Don't Measure Up

The mom laboring under this impression falls short of her own standards. Desiring approval, she performs at a higher level. When feelings of inadequacy surface, she believes she has two options. Either she has to give up, or she has to try harder by being "more": *more* sensitive, *more* financially generous, *more* cheerful. She believes that if she reaches a loftier standard—attending church *more,* dieting *more,* studying *more*—she just *might* earn God's grudging acceptance. Yet all the *mores* in the world eventually fail, taking her back to square one. One single mom expressed the same idea:

With my kids I feel like I never do enough. Will I ever be able to sit down on the inside and just "be"? Be satisfied. Be at peace. Be relaxed that my sufficiency comes from Christ alone.

How can this mom learn that depending on her performance to win people's and God's approval keeps her on the gerbil wheel of running, doing, going, and getting nowhere fast?

I Am Trapped

Wounded people feel stuck in a revolving door of poor decisions, believing they have no control over the direction of their lives. Such was the case with Shannon, a mother of three who came to our ministry messed up, doped up, and ready to commit suicide.

I grew up in a great home. Don't ask me why I made so many horrible choices. I was an addict to punishment. I married a man at eighteen that I didn't love and gave birth to my first son while being heavily involved in alcohol, cocaine, and methamphetamines. After my husband struck a blow to our son's head, he served time in prison for child endangerment charges while I continued my ravagement with other men. After my husband's release from prison, I stayed in his web of manipulation, a prisoner to my own wounds, with me starting physical fights at home just to get the beatings behind me so I could enjoy the rest of the evening. On my thirty-second birthday, I sat in an abortion clinic, having lost temporary custody of my son. How many emotional assaults would it take for God to get my attention? I loathed my shame, but how could I live without it?

Friend, is it possible for the Shannons of the world to shift from self-contempt to God's pardon and unconditional love? How can this prison be escaped?

I Carry an Inflated Sense of Responsibility

Do you feel as though it is your God-given assignment to monitor and fix the emotional state of everyone around you? Are you so busy handling everyone else's emotions that your own get swept under the rug until the kids graduate? Does your sense of wellbeing come from externals: the kids' behavior, cleanliness of your house, peace in your relationships? Do you do everything possible to avoid stressful situations but find yourself in the crossfire of conflict anyway? If so, you are worn to a nub, entombed in your efforts to rescue those around you while dying in the process. Sheer survival demands a lot of work. But you protest, "If I don't forewarn, counsel, and scrutinize, who will?"

How can this mom break out of her safeguarding mode? What would it look like for her to redefine everyone's role, including her own?

Inflatables from Above

Shame and guilt bubble up as unavoidable parts of the human experience, but we don't have to drown in their tide. God has provided life jackets for those on a "vessel" in distress. Even a toddler understands the value of a floaty. How can we take hold of God's rescue plan and rise above the vigorous rip current of shame and guilt?

Floaty #1—Recognize the Undertow of Your Belief System

What data determines how you view and respond to God, yourself, and others? This information creates a grid in which your feelings and personal identity take shape. Your emotions are sifted through either a shame-based filter or a Christ-based filter. Identifying your emotional strainer helps you understand your feelings. Which of the following best describes your colander of life?

Shame-based filter
- Self-image comes from past mistakes, disgust with personal appearance, and destructive habits.
- Wellbeing is built upon the crumbled pieces of yesterday's memories.
- Rejection and a disappointment with others prevail.
- Life is lived out of the soul (a fleshly mind, a skewed will, unbridled emotions).

Christ-based filter
- Self-image comes from God's opinion and trust in the Holy Spirit to bring change.
- Wellbeing is built upon God's unconditional love and tomorrow's anticipated victories.
- Hope and an expectation of God to work everything together for good prevail.
- Life finds release through the Holy Spirit ruling over the mind, will, and emotions.

Our belief system serves as a life rudder. If it is corroded, it leads to a shipwreck of faith and hampers the healing process. If it is grounded in who we are in Christ, it enables God to take charge of our emotions so they won't take charge of us.

Floaty #2—Recollect If This Is True Conviction or False Guilt
Someone, not something, drives our guilt. It is either assigned by our enemy, the accuser who stands before God day and night, reminding the Father of our shortcomings, or it is allowed by God. Knowing the motive behind each charge determines what we are to do.

- *False Guilt/Satan's Tool:* This leads one into the swamp of ill repute through allegations, disapproval, and loss of personal integrity.
- *True Conviction/God's Tool:* This leads one into a right relationship with the Father through confession, cleansing, and a restored fellowship with Him.

Just because we *feel* guilty doesn't mean we *are* guilty.

Therefore, deciphering which of the two rumbles in our spirits demands cross-examining each accusation with the "Guilt Test." Do I feel disgraced? Do I feel a nudge of blame for my failures? Is this thought "me-centered," with no redeeming value? That is false guilt, originating from the devil.

On the other hand, godly remorse originates from the Holy Spirit leading us to a confession about our wrongdoing. It provides an internal cleansing of not only our guilt and shame but also their cause: sin. True conviction is always God-centered, and it leads to repentance and restoration with the Father. It never leaves us with a personal sense of denunciation. True conviction decrees God's adoration. False guilt decrees self-condemnation.

Floaty #3—Restore Fellowship with Christ Through Confession

As followers of Christ, we intellectually understand that Jesus died for our sins, but we struggle with the residue they leave behind: feelings of shame, guilt, and inferiority. What use is it that Christ died for our sins if their effects pound us to death? The enemy does not want us to know the other side of the truth. Yes, our sins were nailed to the cross, but their lingering scum was nailed there, as well. To allow these injurious emotions to destroy us is to say that Christ's work on the cross was not enough, so we must finish it. But Jesus said, "It is finished!" Christ dealt with shame, guilt, inferiority, and all other accusatory emotions on the cross.

Friend, what sin, along with its babies, are you carrying? Grab hold of the power of the cross. Take back the ground you have given to Satan. The Bible confirms that our sin and its effects remain powerless to block our recovery to wholeness. Freedom comes through confessing our wrongdoing and reestablishing a clear conscience. First John 1:9 testifies, *"If we confess our sins, He is faithful and just to forgive us our sins [and its effects] and cleanse us from all unrighteousness."*

No sin is too big for God to wipe away its shame. He waits to restore a clean conscience, and it happens through genuine confession. What does that look like? Confession does not only relieve the conscience, nor is it a bandage to cover our wrongdoing when we know we plan to continue committing the sin. Rather, confession is a godly sorrow that moves us to turn away from temptation. Then we receive God's cleansing. It looks like this (fill in the blanks with your sins and their ruinous emotions):

- My (sin and effect) remain out of sight: *For I, the Lord, put all your sins behind My back.* (Isaiah 38:17)
- My (sin and effect) remain out of mind: *For I, the Lord, remember your sins no more.* (Isaiah 43:25)
- My (sin and effect) remain out of reach: *For I, the Lord, place all sin underfoot and will hurl every iniquity into the sea.* (Micah 7:19b)
- My (sin and effect) remain out of existence: *For I, the Lord, remove your sins as far as the east is from the west.* (Psalm 103:12)

Confession is a life change that restores God's fellowship. True confession throws us a life jacket.

God's three floaties serve their purposes, but they are not the long-term answer for relief from the daunting emotions that plague our souls. We need someone to send a lifeboat and take us to shore. Friend, the rescue vehicle has come: *God's grace.* Will we dare to climb on board?

ABOUNDING IN GOD'S GRACE

After you have suffered for a little while, the God of all grace, who called you to His eternal glory, will Himself restore, support, and strengthen you on a firm foundation.
1 Peter 5:10

I grew up in a Christian home and attended youth camps that taught me about God's love. In my twenties, I served the Lord as a summer missionary to Malaysia. I have been in full-time ministry most of my adult life. I have taught on grace, written on grace, drawn stick figures on grace. Yet, here I am admitting that its magnificence leaves me out-and-out speechless, unable to express its wonder with only words. *(Lord, help me!)* How can one begin to describe the *bounty* of God's goodness in the life of a believer?

We love the idea of receiving both God's grace and mercy. Yet they remain quite different. While mercy withholds a punishment we deserve, grace gives a blessing we don't deserve. Just how great is grace? Consider this. Suppose you got a speeding ticket and appeared before a judge. You were guilty as charged, but he canceled your fine. That is mercy. Yet while you were leaving, the judge pointed to a hot red Mercedes at the curb and handed you the keys. That is grace. The remarkable gift of grace seems too good to be true! It is foreign to us to receive such extravagance with no strings attached. It costs us nothing. It costs *someone else* everything.

What is this blessing called "grace"? It is God's divine assistance that enables us to do with ease what we could never do on our own. It is proof of our ability to bounce high after we hit rock bottom. It is the Father's good pleasure and unmerited favor. Grace covers our wrong, heals our past, empowers our present, and restores our future. Ephesians 2:8 describes its origin: *"For it is by his grace that you are saved through trusting him; it is not your own doing. It is God's gift, not reward for work done."*

Grace covers our wrong, heals our past, empowers our present, and restores our future.

As grateful as we are for this Mercedes, many of us don't know how to "drive it," as far as freeing us from the effects of shame and false guilt. While trying to explain this idea, I was reminded of connect-the-dots pictures. You remember: your pencil travels from dot number one to dot number two and so on until the picture comes into view. But what would happen if you drew from dot four to dot six? Your hidden image would never fully appear because dot five was skipped. In the same manner, the reason why we can't calm our rollercoaster emotions is because we missed a dot. What is that dot?

The Great Exchange

When God looks at His followers, what colors does He see?

Green for envious? Black for sinful? Gray for wishywashy? Because God is holy, anyone who comes into His presence must be sinless, a person who *always* does what is right. Who, then, can set foot in His throne room? Even at our best, the Bible describes our finest deeds as filthy rags.

Jesus Christ is the only perfect One. He took our sins upon Himself at the cross, becoming our substitute that we might stand in God's presence clean and holy. God charged our sinfulness to Christ's account. But God did something else, which remains the key for us to live in a state of emotional peace. Not only did God place our wrongdoings on Christ's ledger, but the Father also credited our account with Christ's perfection. We swapped our sin for His blamelessness. We became partakers of His divine nature. We became right with God as if we had never sinned and always obeyed.[1] Friend, the dot we are overlooking is this: God exchanged our sins for Christ's virtue, the most demonstrative act of grace known to mankind. Only the life, death, and resurrection of Christ offer a valid pathway to freedom from a guilty and shame-filled conscience.

So what color does God see when He looks upon us? Because we are *in* Christ and He is *in* us, God sees our robe of Christ's righteousness, perfectly enlaced with white (His purity) and red (His blood). Like pouring hot water over ice, this robe melts the regrets that left us feeling like failures.

The Blessing Pancake

John 1:16 affirms God's radical heart as a giver. He longs to bestow grace upon grace and blessing upon blessing, one favor piled on top of another with strawberry syrup on top. Who couldn't use a bit of God kindness like that? The Father wants us to experience His plenty. Second Corinthians 9:8 confirms, *"And God is able to make all grace abound to you, so that having all sufficiency in all things at all times, you may abound in every good work."*

I adore the word *abound*. In Greek, it means "to be in excess, to have remaining residue after needs are met."[2] Friend, raise your hand if you would like some of that residue. In what area of your life do you most desire a touch of God's excess? Do you need strength to cope, a release from worry, an answer to prayer?

I love God's promise. It gives so much hope. He has the power to work in our gravest areas of need in such a way that His goodness overflows into our emotional strength, physical stamina, and spiritual wisdom as mothers, employees, and friends. His grace doesn't just make them abound. It makes them superabound!

Let's examine four areas where this kind of grace finds its deepest expression.

Grace Abounds in "How"

As a single mom, one of your greatest enemies begins with the letter *h*. And I don't mean a *husband* or your desire for a *hideout*. The enemy is the fear tucked behind the word *how*.

- *How can I be the kind of woman God desires?*
- *How can I provide more stability for my family?*
- *How can I steady my rollercoaster emotions?*

Around every corner lurks a "how question" concerning our immense inabilities. *Hows* feel terminal. *Hows* feel scary. *Hows* paralyze us.

Krista, a mother of two girls, knew these "hows" well following her husband's suicide.

How could my husband do this to me after we had resolved our problems? How could God let this happen? How could I ever trust God again? How could God heal my friend's family problems but not mine?

What's a mom to do when she is ensnared by a twisted perception of God and wrapped in anger? God understands, and He leads us, like Krista, into His gracious care.

After my three months of shaking my fist at God, I'd had enough. God spoke to me, "Krista, I've been carrying you. It's time to surrender your will to My keeping. When you wrestle against your circumstances, you frustrate the movement of My Spirit by your lack of faith. My grace is sufficient for you. Will you trust My infinite resources?"

As single moms, we often fear that God's provisions are going to run out. What does *sufficient* mean? In Greek, it suggests that God has more than enough "to assist, satisfy, suffice, make strong."[3] Once we know that, in every situation, God is enough, our soul is calmed.

Do we honestly believe that God's storehouse is big enough to sustain our family's needs? Do we trust in His ampleness over our emptiness? Do we cling to His supply over our shortage? Just how vast is His reserve? A tiny fish pondered the same questions after taking multiple gulps of water. "Father, will there be enough water to quench my thirst tomorrow?" With a chuckle, God responded, "Drink away, my precious fish. My ocean is sufficient for you."

In what areas do you desire reassurance that God's resources will never run dry? Do you fear for your finances, career, or relationships? God's sufficiency will always provide. The Father's provisions remain infinite, forever. Krista confirms, *"I've found the sufficiency of my eternal Father. He's more than revealed Himself to me and filled my empty and angry places with His amazing love."*

God's sufficiency will always provide.

Friend, God the Almighty rides through the skies dressed in His majesty to handle your deepest concern. His manifold grace is enough.

Grace Abounds in Surrender

We are our own worst enemies. Why do we focus more on our failures than on God's rescues? Why do we focus more on our wrongs than on God's commitment to making them right? Why do we take personal responsibility for our children's choices? Why do we find it hard to let go of something we did that affects our child? Because we carry that *m* word deep within: motherhood. Whether the guilt is true or false, its sting stays in our systems. And although we know that the robes of righteousness cover us, we still wrestle. One single mom relates, *"Though God has forgiven me, I still feel guilty that my daughter was born with a hole in her heart due to my drug use when pregnant. How do I get over what I did?"* Can you relate? Have you heard your own haunting voices?

- *What was I thinking?*
- *Why didn't I do "this" or "that"?*
- *What could I have done differently?*

Friend, I understand. I experienced remorse whenever I saw my children's little faces and felt that they deserved a "Daddy/Mommy" home. I wondered what I could have done differently to keep their father happy. Every child wants their original parents successfully married, and when we cannot provide that, we feel a degree of sorrow and personal responsibility. Romans 8:28 became my best friend: *"For God causes all things to work together for good, to those who love God and to those who are called according to his purpose."*

Thank the Lord. Although all things aren't "good," God works them together for a higher benefit, one infinitely better than what we originally desired. In other words, God weaves His purposes into our children when we entrust their lives to Him. To "entrust" is a bank term, meaning "to deposit." When we place our "child treasures" into God's safekeeping, He protects our investments. Friend, we need to make more *bank deposits* on a regular basis. They yield dividends both now and for eternity.

How else can we handle guilt? We can talk to God. There are many spiritual disciplines we ought to do, but one we must do: *pray.* Prayer gets our problems out of our hearts and into God's hands. Grace abounds in prayer! It is the central avenue God uses to transform us. It trains the soul to realign our perspective with God's.

- Prayer summons God's presence into the circumstance.
- Prayer transfers worries to a higher source.
- Prayer unfurls hope when there is none.
- Prayer puts God's thoughts in our minds.
- Prayer drives us to God when we have nowhere else to go.
- Prayer makes God's presence real.

Prayer gets our problems out of our hearts and into God's hands.

Pray without ceasing.

Lord, I am not a perfect mom. Have mercy on me where I have failed or fallen short. Give me the courage to trust You when I don't see the results I desire. Remind me that Your grace is more than enough and though my children might not receive my instruction well for the time being, they are powerless against my prayers. Lord, I testify that You are higher than my greatest fear and wiser than my deepest lack. For the rest of my days I will speak well of You concerning every trial, as You have promised that Your grace produces miracles for those who trust in You. Amen.

Pray. Just pray. When life knocks you to your knees, stay there. Satan can't keep God from answering your prayers, but he can keep you from asking. So pray. Surrendered prayers unlock the floodgate of God's boundless grace.

Grace Abounds in Second Chances

What is the most shameful thing you have ever done? Have you ever disgraced yourself as a leader in front of your entire sphere of influence? Have you committed adultery with a married man and secretly plotted to murder his wife? Have you covered your shame by lying about your sin? King David understands these scenarios well. He did all of those evil deeds. Yet God not only gave him a second chance, but He placed Jesus the Messiah in David's lineage. When we seek God out of a spirit of contrition, the Father extends His grace by making our mess His message.

I rarely meet a woman who at one time or another has not pleaded with God for a clean slate once again. Laura, a single mother of two, is familiar with the feeling.

As a child, I prayed every night year after year for the abuse to stop, but it didn't. As a teenager I prayed for help dealing with an unwanted pregnancy and ended up being raped by a friend's father and another man. As an adult, I covered the pain with an addiction: shopping. Running up over half a million dollars on my credit cards, I continued the downward spiral: spending, stealing, lying, then spending more. For what? Designer labels to make me feel better? Anything to cover up my past sexual abuse, two abortions, four miscarriages, divorce, and infidelity. At thirty-five years old I found myself serving time in a federal prison.

Do I know guilt? It wrenched my soul to watch my husband carry my three- and five-year-old away from the prison bars with their arms stretched forth screaming as they left, "Mommy, Mommy, hold me!" Yet, God's grace found me there, covering my shame with His forgiveness and affection. Today I'm a free woman in more ways than one. I entered the penitentiary a woman of shameful disgust. I exited a woman adorned as God's princess and delight. I'm living proof of the power of God's wondrous grace. Only Christ makes all things new.

What happens when we receive God's complete forgiveness? What Satan meant for evil transforms into God's highest and best. It changes us. It impacts others. Channing, Laura's daughter, writes:

Mommy, there is never a more beautiful mother than you. Even though you messed up and went to prison, you're the "bomb"! Thank you for showing me what Jesus looks like.

Friend, when Christ's fullness and healing power flow through us, it is the "bomb," an anointing from God's throne of power, testifying to His explosive desire to set us free. So celebrate. God gives each of us chance after chance.

Grace Abounds in Recycling

I keep a container of plastic bottles in my garage to be placed at the curb for recycling. What a genius idea that our trash can be reprocessed into something useful! That is the way shame and guilt and other heartaches work. God recycles them into something beautiful.

John Newton, the author of the hymn "Amazing Grace," never forgot his depravity as a slave trader. Instead of wallowing in his guilt, he took it to the cross and left it there. To the end of his life he remembered both his sin and the gospel. On his deathbed at eighty two, he commented, "My memory is nearly gone, but I remember two things: that I am a great sinner and that Christ is a great Savior."[4]

Time and space do not limit God's grace. It is our greatest

advantage in life, so broad we cannot wrap our minds around it, yet so close we feel its gentle embrace. It is God's kiss for every single mom.

Grace:

- transforms failures into fortunes.
- turns fear into peace.
- recasts mistakes as miracles.
- restores lost dreams to uncharted opportunities.
- restyles a garment of despair into a robe of righteousness.

We ask, "What's so amazing about grace?" Friend, what isn't amazing about grace?

Whispers from Jesus

You have carried your guilt too long. Accept your past. Accept the choices you made. Accept the consequences, and entrust them into My care. As long as you cling to your regrets, you impede My presence and frustrate the release of My power. But when you let go, My grace flows into your need. When trapped in the cloak of guilt, hear My whisper, "I cherish you, My love."

Silent Reflection

1. What makes you feel guilty?
2. What voices not listed in the "swells of shame" section do you hear?
3. Explain the shame-based and Christ-based filters. Which one do you use?
4. What happens when you envision your robe of righteousness?
5. What ministered to you in this chapter?

Gentle Respite for the Soul

God Forgives

Isaiah 6:7—*Your guilt is taken away and your sin atoned for.*

Psalm 32:5—*I acknowledged my sin and did not cover up my iniquity. I confessed my transgressions to the Lord and He forgave the guilt of my sin.*

God Makes New

Psalm 51:10—*Create in me a clean heart, O God, and renew a steadfast spirit within me.*

Ezekiel 18:31—*Cast away from you all transgressions and throw off the load of your past misdeeds. Make yourselves a new heart and a new spirit.*

God Supplies Grace

2 Corinthians 12:9-10—*"My grace is sufficient for you, for My power is made perfect in weakness." Therefore, I will boast all the more gladly about my weaknesses, so that Christ's power may rest on me. That is why, for Christ's sake, I delight in weaknesses, in insults, in hardships, in persecutions, in difficulties. For when I am weak, then I am strong.*

Hebrews 4:16—*Let us then approach the throne of grace with confidence, so that we may receive mercy and find grace to help us in our time of need.*

CHAPTER EIGHT

From the Rubble of Discouragement to Expectation of Victory

Why are you in despair, O my soul [emotions], *and why have you become disturbed within me? Hope in God, for I shall again praise Him for the help of His presence.*
Psalm 42:5

Every person wants their longings fulfilled, desiring that good awaits in their tomorrows. It is built into the fabric of our natures. It is called hope. But what happens when we are tired, fainthearted, and lose perspective? You are a single mom, after all.

Of all of the emotions on your rollercoaster, *this* one feels the most debilitating: discouragement. At every twirl and whirl, raising children alone can drain joy and strength. Do any of these appear on your list of distresses?

- Dealing with the children's demands for attention, sympathy, and transportation
- Coming home from a full day's work only to start the night shift
- Explaining why the children can't have what "so and so" has
- Finding adult conversation in which to share interests, worries, and joys
- Discovering a church home that understands your plight
- Dealing with household issues: the kitchen faucet is dripping, the car is making a strange noise
- Ignoring the stares in the grocery store because your child is throwing a fit and you are too tired to deal with it
- Apologizing incessantly for (unavoidably) arriving late

to work, missing work (again) because little Max has a runny nose, and not feeling adequate for your children

No wonder single motherhood is hard! Handling one disappointment after another crushes the spirit. The Bible teaches that delayed hope makes the heart sick and feeble. Nehemiah understands anguish. He was an Old Testament character facing the seemingly impossible task of rebuilding the walls of Jerusalem after Israel was seized by the Babylonians. God charged Nehemiah with the most colossal remodeling project in history. How could one man carry out such a massive task?

You ought to know. God has appointed you to gather up the pieces of your life and restore the walls of your own city. Yet take heart. God would no more leave the Jewish nation in shambles than He would leave you in permanent disrepair. The same God who rehabilitated a damaged fort into a mighty fortress promises to refurbish your shack of discouragement into a castle of praise. God is the one who can bring back to life that which looks dead. You are not defeated. You are not crushed on every side. You are not pressed down. God works even when you don't think He is, and when you are down to nothing, *He is up to something.* Never does the Father allow His children to remain in permanent disarray.

When you are down to nothing, He is up to something.

Intensive—But Not Impossible

It was likely a sultry afternoon when King Artaxerxes of Persia inquired why Nehemiah, his closest attendant, paced the palace sadly. Nehemiah never dreamed his homeland would face the shame of being undefended. War left masses of debris before the destroyed wall. The chaotic state of the city and their inability to rebuild the empire shamed the Jews.

But with the king's blessing and God Almighty at the helm, Nehemiah returned to Jerusalem to restore the beams of the citadel, reconstruct the city walls, and reunite the people. Halfway through the renovation, however, Nehemiah encountered what you face in your restoration mission, too: fatigue, frustration, and failure.

Overcome with Fatigue

What happens when you work 24/7 with no break or personal boundaries? Ask the workers rebuilding the Jewish community. Nehemiah 4:10 reports, *"And the strength of the laborers was failing."* They felt as though they couldn't go on one day longer.

Perhaps this sounds all too familiar. With no in-house spouse to share the responsibilities, it is easy to overtax your physical strength and want to give up: *I'm sick and tired of this.* Or maybe you feel, with a twinge of self-pity, as if you have no control over your fatigue: *Somebody has to pull the weight of this family uphill.* While I am not minimizing the reality of your exhaustion nor suggesting that you ignore your doctor's orders, I do know that God has given us a body that responds best to kind treatment. Our Creator knows how we tick. He made us. But for many single moms, caring for their bodies is the last priority on their emergency list. They know that something is out of whack, but they push it off until tomorrow. As single moms, we sometimes fail to think reasonably. For example, would we ignore a blinking oil light in our car? Or would we disregard the fire alarm if it woke us up at three o'clock? Of course not, so why do we snub our body's messages that it needs a tune-up: rollercoaster emotions, paranoia, a victim mentality, escapism, suicidal thoughts?

God's instruction manual, the Bible, contains a maintenance schedule to keep us from blowing fuses, getting flat tires, and emptying the gas from our tanks. In Genesis, the Father commanded His people to rest on the Sabbath. Why should we cease our crazy schedules? Why should we put agendas aside? Because during this "timeout" from the rat race, God supernaturally refuels us, giving us the energy and drive to accomplish ten times more than if we had worked ten times harder without Him. Physical rest and meditation on God's Word infuse spiritual vigor.

I understand your plight. It's easy to lose your sense of sanity and balance in the pandemonium. As a single mom, I often reminded myself, *Pam, if you avoid God's "timeout corner," there are consequences to pay: loss of judgment, loss of productivity, loss of spiritual vision and power.* I needed all of those. Resting in God directed my spiritual antennas so that I could hear His voice, gain perspective, and realign my spirit with His. God spoke: *Pam, your body is My holy dwelling place. How can I work through it if it's waning from lack of sleep, exercise, and a proper diet?* I looked at myself in the mirror. I was stunned by its overlooked abuse. No wonder I felt fatigued.

Often, single moms view body care as selfish because there are more important things to do. LaTonjia, a single mom with one son, writes:

My life coach said I needed to pamper myself weekly in order to keep my sanity. So I made an appointment for a facial. It was lovely: music relaxing, candle burning, lights dimming. But I couldn't relax. I felt guilty knowing I was wasting one and a half hours when I should have been cleaning house or working on my graduate project.

Does this sound familiar? Friend, heed the warning: "get apart" before you "come apart." Just take care of yourself. The dust, the dogs, and the dirty laundry can wait. They will be there tomorrow, but you might not be.

Overwhelmed with Frustration

No doubt, when you leave for work, your famous last words to your teenager resound: "When I get home, this house better be clean!" Nothing weighs us down more than physical and emotional clutter. Nehemiah's workers understood. In Nehemiah 4:10, they grumbled, *"There is so much rubbish. We can't begin to finish this wall."* Focusing on the stone structures hampered their stamina and belief that God would complete the assignment. You understand such boulders. You have your own pyramids blocking your field of vision:

- My child is not getting any better.
- I have prayed and prayed and nothing is happening.
- My personal debris multiplies daily.
- I am cried out, stressed out, and burned out.

Discouragement and its first cousin, depression, seem insurmountable. But they are not. By sifting and sorting, we can discover where the frustration originates and take the root to God. I remember driving home from school as a single mom one snowy afternoon with a spirit of restlessness. Why was I bothered? I didn't know. I pleaded, "God, what's wrong with me?" He revealed my problem: I had been building my "Life's Not Fair Wall." By submitting to my *condition* rather than my *position* of authority over my emotions, I was trapped. Brick by brick, it enclosed me. It would have been much easier if I had never begun the construction project in the first place. So where do we start in tearing down these walls of disappointment? Begin by examining three perpetrators that fuel frustration.

1. Doing Life My Way

There is only one road to walking out of discouragement or enduring it with God's grace, and that is falling under the control of the Holy Spirit and obeying whatever instructions He gives. The Bible teaches that we reap what we sow, more than we sow, and later than we sow. When our disobedience of God's Word becomes a lifestyle without a spirit of confession, consequences enmesh us in a web of discomfort. We might be flustered because we have left God out of the picture.

2. Leaning On My Own Speculations

For most of us, God doesn't act fast enough. We are impatient. We want solutions now: we desired a mate yesterday; we need direction tonight. The problem is that we don't trust in God's timing or faithfulness to provide. When we're discouraged, there is only one place to run: the promises of God's Word. In my single-parent life, Proverbs 3:5-6 found a home on countless post-it-notes stuck to various spots: my bathroom mirror, steering wheel, desk at work, kids' bedframes. If it could stick, it stuck. This verse encouraged me to stop trying to figure everything out and relax in God's care: *"Lean on, trust in, be confident in the Lord with all your heart and mind and do not rely on your own insight or understanding. In all your ways know, recognize and acknowledge Him, and He will direct and make straight your paths."* Indeed, self-calculation released to God's calculation produces rest and peace.

3. Disregarding the Shaping of God's Hand

Not all discouragement is bad. It might reveal that God is at work. In a sense, it serves a valuable purpose. Hebrews 12:5 says, *"For whom God loves, He chastens."* Chastening can feel like anxiety or distress. One single mom commented, *"What used to bring me fulfillment doesn't anymore. What's going on?"* She might be in the garden house with God and not know it. Our loving Father, the Vinedresser, uses our difficulties to prune us so that we might produce more spiritual fruit.

How is God pruning you? He might be trimming off bad attitudes or snipping away the things you think are best in your life. Or perhaps He is asking you to give up the right to be married again or to stop dating a man who isn't good for you. The Father prunes what is closest to us—that thing that rates higher than our desire to please Him. Whatever the case, the last time I checked, God's shears hurt! Pruning can easily be mislabeled as discouragement rather than the whittling of God's hands. Whatever God is asking you to do may seem difficult, but when you yield to His refining, you receive a hundred times more than you ever imagined. Remember the Law of Harvest: *more.* God's "more" boomerangs out of one simple act of obedience. Are you ready to say yes to the Vinedresser?

Overspent in Failure

For me, one of the hardest parts of being a single mother was feeling like a loser. I had always been successful in my relationships and endeavors. I was a cheerleader, popular student, and on the student council. When my marriage fell apart and innocent children were caught in the wake, I felt like the scarlet-letter-bearing woman of shame. In Nehemiah 4:10, the bricklayers understood ruin and defeat: *"and we ourselves are unable to rebuild the wall."* By relying on their own strength, the workers faced the humiliation of Israel's defeat.

We each have our reasons for feeling that we have failed. But we are not failures. God looks at defeat differently than we do. What is the truth about failure?

- Failure is not a door that closes but a gate that opens with useful life lessons we would not have received otherwise.
- Failure does not define our identity. It is only something that happened to us. We determine if our past or marital status is synonymous with the word *failure*.
- Failure is not something we can escape. We live in a fallen world. We made mistakes in the past. We will make more tomorrow.
- Failure is not the worst thing that could happen. Doubting that God will do something useful out of it kills more dreams than failure ever could.
- Failure is not permanent. It is a process we pass through, an experience that trains us to know God more intimately.

Failure is nothing more than a tool in God's hands that fashions us for better things. Friend, I am most sympathetic about what brought you to this place. But God is not finished with you yet. There is purpose in setbacks. If God subtracted one letdown, one misfortune, one boo-boo, one calamity, one failure, then you would be less than the woman you are now and ill equipped for where God is taking you. So do not be discouraged. Your attitude toward failure determines God's altitude in making good use of it.

Failure is nothing more than a tool in God's hands that fashions us for better things.

If God subtracted one letdown, one misfortune, one boo-boo, one calamity, one failure, then you would be less than the woman you are now and ill equipped for where God is taking you.

God—the Restorer of Lost Dreams

It is a tragedy that many single mothers give up on the brink of seeing God transform cobblestones into chateaux of splendor and trials into towers of His might. Nehemiah's men were tempted to lose heart, but they didn't. Nor did they listen to the threats of their neighboring enemies. With a sledgehammer in one hand and a solid resolve to trust God in the other, each persevered. And a phenomenon emerged on the pages of history: God supernaturally enabled them to complete the wall in only fifty-four days! Such a feat remains one of the most awe-inspiring displays of God's intervention in the ancient world.

What would happen if we abandoned ourselves to an Almighty God who still performs miracles? Are we ready for Him to make history within our own city walls? Friend, He is restoring you at this moment. I know it. I feel it.

Cross over the threshold with me, and let's receive His grace.

EXPECTATION OF VICTORY

For I know the plans I have for you, plans for welfare and not for calamity, to give you a future and a hope. . . . Seek Me and I will be found by you. . . . I will restore your fortunes.
Jeremiah 29:11-14

I love the sound of the word "victory." It makes me envision God winning our battles in the places where we most plead for a blessing.

- *Lord, provide for my children.*
- *Lord, make my single motherhood count for Your Kingdom.*
- *Lord, plant Your victory banner over this household.*

These are what we desire. The Bible teaches that we have not because we ask not. But I believe something else, too. We have not because we anticipate not. I remember when the Lord introduced me to the principle of expectation.

The Dining-Room Revelation

I collapsed in my dining-room chair in the darkness at five o'clock in the morning, traumatized and numb with disbelief. I had been married for ten years. Jason and Sara were toddlers. My husband and I faithfully attended church, where I was teaching God's Word to college students. But life threw an unforeseen curve my way. My husband wanted a divorce. I was too shocked to cry, too dazed to think straight, too disoriented to even know my name. I slumped in my chair like a ragdoll.

As I stared outside the window, the sun came up over the roof of the house across the street, beaming on me like a mysterious flashlight. The Bible character Saul came to mind and how God appeared to him on the road to Damascus with a light so intense it likely buckled his knees. In my stupor, I begged of God, *Lord, speak to me.* In my fog I waited for His message. And God spoke. It wasn't an audible sound but an inner voice. I felt God's presence within me.

Pam, I am with you. Start keeping journals. Stay close to Me continually. Your sorrows are not in vain but allowed and purposeful. I am going to raise you up to speak to thousands of women about what My grace and power can do through one single mom fully yielded to Me. Expect Me to do what I have said. Expect My faithfulness. Expect Me to come alongside. You are not dead in your distresses but alive in My plan, alive in our joint venture.

As I staggered to the kitchen *half-dead* while pondering that I was *alive,* God revealed part two of His prophecy through a vision. He showed me how His mission would unfold in the years to come. Friend, that was in the 1990s. I have journaled the journey. Today I praise God for fulfilling a hundredfold every ounce of that vision with a national ministry that has blessed thousands of women.

Does God still speak to single mothers as He did to me? Does He still transform wounds of sadness into witnesses of hope? Does God still use flashlights to impart divine aspirations? He does. In fact, His penlight beams on you now. Beware. These next few moments might serve as your morning dining-room encounter.

Celestial Visions

Hope—we pray for it, live for it, and die without it. The Bible confirms our desire for encouragement, purpose, and life from God. Proverbs 29:18 says, *"Where there is no vision, the people perish."*

What is this vision that we need? It is a divine revelation offering forgiveness for yesterday, endurance for today, and guidance for tomorrow. This hope comes through incarnating His Word, communing through prayer, and worshipping Him in song and praise. These Heavenly encounters originate from an actual place that governs and supplies our Christian life. It is where Jesus sits at the right hand of God, serving as the author, initiator, and dispenser of hope. Christ's hope is with us. His hope is in us. In 1 Peter 1:3, it says, *"We have been born again to a living hope through the resurrection of Christ."* Jesus Christ, our living hope, sustains us when we need reinforcement, supports us when we need a listening ear, and stabilizes us when we need a hand through the storm. Friend, no matter what you are facing, *you have hope.*

Hope Comes Alive

So how do we keep this hope alive even in our troubles? Just as God instructed me in that dining-room chair, we expect His faithfulness:

- We *expect* God to transform us into the image of His Son.
- We *expect* God to work our singleness for good.
- We *expect* God to "father" the children.
- We *expect* God to abide with us.
- We *expect* God to lead the way.
- We *expect* God to take care of the details.

We never stop expecting God's goodness to prevail. Why? Because we are *alive* in His purposes, *alive* in His plan, *alive* in His testimony. We are first and foremost spiritual beings; therefore, shouldn't we strive to live in that realm? So how can we exercise single motherhood on that level? We choose to live, not drag ourselves around as if we were half-dead. Three avenues lead to hope.

1. The Holy Spirit's Supremacy

Every emotion either benefits or destroys. We choose how our emotions will either work for or against us. They don't control us. We control them through God's Spirit. When we plunge down the rollercoaster track plagued with worry, fear, and regret, we separate ourselves from God's peace and fullness. But God has a better plan. A life filled with the Holy Spirit stabilizes rollercoaster emotions. In Ephesians 3:16, Paul offers instruction for a spirit-generated life: *"Be strengthened with power by God's Spirit in our inner man."* What is our inner man and how does it relate to our emotions? We find the answer by understanding the nature of our design. We are a three-part being.

A life filled with the Holy Spirit stabilizes rollercoaster emotions.

At salvation, when Christ's Spirit, life, and power dwell within us, He enters our deepest core, called the inner man. Outside of the inner man is the soul (the outer man), the place that houses our thoughts, will, and emotions. Outside of the outer man is the body (the outermost man). However, it is the inner man (the Spirit of God) that desires release and authority.

In other words, God's Holy Spirit that indwells our innermost being yearns for freedom, so that we might experience God's presence and be useful for His purposes. Yet, the Spirit must first pass through the hard shell of our flesh and the worldly thoughts that deprive the Spirit of God's fullest measure and thwart His activity. When we submit to the workings of God, our will breaks, creating a channel for the Holy Spirit to come forth and refine us.

It is then that the inner man holds absolute sway over the outer man.

If we want to be vessels fit for the Master's use and live in a hope that God is working our circumstances for a higher purpose, we must place our souls under the control and restraint of the Spirit of God. Friend, submission matters. Watchman Nee confirms, "God's Spirit is released according to the degree of our brokenness. For indeed, God breaks us to release us."[1]

So where does true hope find its strength? John 3:30 explains, *"For I [the soul/outer man] must decrease, and He [the Spirit/inner man] must increase."*

2. Obedience

One of my favorite single-mom stories in the Bible revolves around the widow from Zarephath in 1 Kings 17. God had instructed Elijah to go to her house for food and shelter. Upon entering the city gate, he found her gathering sticks and asked for a drink of water and a biscuit.

She replied, *"As the Lord lives, I have no bread, only a handful of flour in a jar and a little oil; you found me scratching together just enough firewood to make a last meal for my son and me. After we eat, we will die."*

Then Elijah asked a preposterous favor. *"Make me a biscuit first and afterward you can make one for yourself and your son. For the Lord of Israel says your bowl of flour will not become empty nor will your jar of oil run dry."*

What would you have done if God's man stepped into your crisis and asked you to trust Him with such extravagance? How many of us would have given a perfect stranger (even if he was Elijah) our last biscuit with a starving child at hand? This single mother understood the strain of being the sole caretaker in less than favorable conditions. But 1 Kings 17:15-16 recounts, *"Yet she went right off and prepared the biscuit, just as Elijah asked. And it turned out as he said—daily thereafter she received food for her and her family."*

What is the spiritual principle? Blessings follow obedience. Obedience is the outward sign that displays the inward source in charge. I wonder what the widow's life would have looked like the next day if she had told God's man to hit the road. Friend, so much is at stake in your choice to do life God's way: your emotional health, children's stability, future prosperity. Obedience to God's Word is the key to every door you pray that God will open. Notice how obedience puts God to work.

Blessings follow obedience.

Obedience places a hedge of protection around your family. Remember how God placed a security fence around Job when he obeyed? In Job 1:9-10, Satan asked God, *"Have You not made a hedge about him and his household and all sides and blessed the work of his hands? Remove Your protection and watch what he does."* What is a hedge and why do we need one? It is an invisible spiritual barrier or type of enclosure installed by God to protect us from spiritual attacks. God is the watchman of the hedge, and though He might remove it temporarily as He did in Job's case, He always has a higher purpose in mind for our benefit.

Obedience transforms our little into God's much. Luke 16:10 says, *"He that is faithful in that which is least is faithful also in much."* We may think it doesn't matter how we handle the little that we have. But our actions define our characters as stewards. Our fidelity is reflected not by the amount entrusted to us but by how we handle it. The habit we form dealing with the small stuff is the habit we take with us to the big stuff. Single mothers often testify to me, "God is leading me into public ministry someday." "Terrific," I reply. But are they obeying God now in the other areas—relationships, parenting, finances?

Obedience summons God's attention. He remembered the widow's obedience after she gave Elijah the last bite of food. A few verses later, her son dies. After the widow begs Elijah for help, he lays his body over the corpse three times, asking God to raise the boy to life. In 1 Kings 17:24, the Scripture reports, *"Then Elijah carried the son downstairs from the loft and gave him to the widow. 'Here. Your son is alive!'"* Why did God restore the widow's child? Could it be He rewarded the mother for her previous obedience? We don't know, nor do we understand why God answers some prayers with a *yes* and others with a *no*. But we can take heart in knowing that not one gesture of faithfulness on our part goes unnoticed. Scripture promises that every act of submission works on our behalf, and we ultimately receive an eternal reward.

Friend, the blessings God offers when we obey Him should throw us to our knees in praise and thanksgiving. God longs to give, wills to give, plans to give. What is God saying to you about surrendering every area of your single-motherhood life to Him?

3. God's Almighty Power

Every single mom needs Jeremiah 32:17 tucked inside her hope chest: *"O Sovereign Lord, You have made the heavens and earth by Your great power. Nothing is too difficult for You."* It inspires our limited imaginations with the idea that maybe—just maybe—God is bigger than our greatest fears and mightier than our toughest strongholds. Being a single parent remains the hardest assignment imaginable, but you can take courage in the fact that, no matter what you are facing and how much life hurts, God can help.

- No problem is too complex for Him to solve.
- No loss is too great for Him to overcome.
- No passion is too strong for Him to subdue.
- No misery is too deep for Him to relieve.
- No foe is too robust for Him to conquer.
- No mistake is too grave for Him to forgive.
- No prayer is too hard for Him to answer.
- No dream is too big for Him to fulfill.

C. H. Spurgeon spoke of God's invincibility:

He sits on no buttressed throne and leans on no assisting arm. His court is not maintained by courtiers, nor does it borrow its splendor from His creatures. He is Himself the great central Source and Originator of all power.

How is it possible to wrap our human minds around such an

all-powerful God? I recall wondering one day after my husband left, *God, if You're really all powerful, what can You do with my life now? I'm scarred forever.* It wasn't until I realized that God willed to do mighty things through my weaknesses and my past that I began to wear God's eyeglasses. He willed for me to succeed. He willed it for His renown and glory.

What happens when we believe God's plan for good in our lives? The fog lifts; the heart rises up; the "Son" breaks forth. We become God's little princess in the process and everything changes.

- We forget what pain lies behind us and press into the now, treasuring each day's memories.
- We remember that when we value the good that God gives us, He prepares us to receive more.
- We photograph God's bigger picture in our hearts and how He desires to bring it to pass.
- We fix our eyes on Jesus and view our difficulties as purposeful, allowed by God.
- We embrace life's cycles, called seasons, knowing "this too shall pass" (even though we might not want it to change).
- We talk about expectations rather than experiences— envisioning God's promise for a future and a hope.
- We exult that our faith is based upon how much God has wrought in our lives.
- We celebrate through worshipping, singing, and rejoicing in God's love.

Jennifer, a single mom with two girls, encourages:

Moms, God's love for us is unfailing. He doesn't take naps. He doesn't go on vacations. He never forgets, abuses, or abandons us. There is a place within our hearts where only we can exist with Him, a blessed spot of unconditional acceptance, comfort, and rest. The world cannot take it away because the world doesn't own it. In Christ we are becoming more than we ever thought possible, and we're receiving more blessings than we could ever have obtained on our own. As we seek Jesus with all our hearts, we'll find Him, and we, along with our children, will never be the same!

Beloved friend, God is raising an army of single moms like Jennifer across this planet to find spiritual and emotional wholeness in Christ. You are one of them. So take heart. Advance with God's forgiveness behind you, His grace before you, and His power beneath you. Always remember:

You belong to Jesus Christ. He is for you,
your children, your dreams.
He is able to do all things in you and through you.
All that He is able to do, He promises to do.
His love is inexhaustible, His generosity immeasurable,
His grace incalculable.
His benevolence longs to encompass you,
comfort you, empower you.
His blessings cannot be contained, for they are more than your
mind can envision and more than your heart can hold.
This is the God who is for you.
This is the God who enables you.
This is the God who loves you.

*Now may the God of hope fill you with all joy and peace in believing
that you may abound in hope by the power of the Holy Spirit.*
Romans 15:13

Whispers from Jesus

You are experiencing wholeness in a way you have never known before. I am restoring the years the locust has eaten and making everything new. I am increasing your honor. By My physical stripes, you are spiritually and emotionally healed. You have what you need for life and godliness. Nothing limits you nor will any act perpetrated against you thwart My plan. You are alive and well. When you feel discouraged, hear My whisper, "I cherish you, My love."

Silent Reflection

1. Study the diagram of the inner man/outer man/outermost man and explain how the Holy Spirit wins out over our rollercoaster emotions.

2. Read Jeremiah 29:11-14. What does God ask you to do? What does He promise?
3. In what areas of obedience do you need God's strength?
4. Read Psalm 71. Its theme is: *You will restore my life again.* Share your thoughts.
5. What nugget of hope will you take away from this chapter? What will you take away from this book?

Gentle Respite for the Soul

God Blesses

Ephesians 3:20-21—*Now to Him who is able to do exceedingly abundantly beyond all that we ask or think, according to the power that works within us, to Him be the glory.*

Psalm 84:11—*For the Lord God is a sun and shield; the Lord bestows favor and honor; no good thing does He withhold from those whose walk is blameless.*

God Promises

1 Thessalonians 5:24—*Faithful is He who calls you, and He will bring it to pass.*

Hebrews 10:23—*Let us hold unswervingly to the hope we profess, for He who promised is faithful.*

God Endures

Psalm 145:13—*Your kingdom is an everlasting kingdom, and Your dominion endures through all generations. The Lord is faithful to all His promises and loving toward all He has made.*

1 Peter 1:25—*But the word of the Lord stands forever.*

Conclusion

We have come to the end of our rollercoaster ride, and what an adventure we have experienced! Look where we have been. We whirled past devastation, climbed the hill of fear, flown over anger and bitterness, crossed the bridge of anxiety, held on tight in the tunnel of loneliness, swung beneath the rails of low self-worth, looped around and around guilt, and come out on the other side of discouragement. What an accomplishment! I think I'm beginning to like rollercoasters now.

Friend, I leave you with a few last words of hope. You matter. You make a difference, and God is preparing you this season for the next. He is allowing you to experience your difficulty so that you might learn greater dependence on Him and discover His faithfulness. Philippians 1:6 remains my favorite single-mother verse: *"For I am confident of this very thing, that He who began a good work in you will perfect it until the day of Christ."*

God is at work whether you see it or not. Nothing can thwart the Father's good plan when you yield yourself to Him. Your struggle is not in vain. It conforms you to the image of His Son. It models righteousness to your children. It prepares you for your future, both here on earth and in eternity. As Galatians 6:9 says, *"Do not grow weary in doing good, for in due season you will reap a harvest if you do not grow weary or lose heart."* Single motherhood is hard, but it is an opportunity to witness a God who performs great works in those who seek Him with the ultimate purpose of reflecting His goodness and beauty.

So onward and upward you go. Enjoy your rollercoaster ride, and to God be all the glory.

Single motherhood—it's a wondrous adventure.

Notes

Chapter 1

1. *Webster's Unabridged Dictionary* (New York: Random House, 1987), 543.

2. Numbers 11:10-14.

3. 1 Kings 19:4, 19:10.

4. Job 3:11, 3:16.

5. *Strong's Concordance,* G4053, 57.

Chapter 2

1. John MacArthur Commentary—Matthew 8-15 (Chicago: The Moody Bible Institute, 1987), 440.

2. *Webster's Unabridged Dictionary,* 464.

3. My paraphrase of Matthew 6:25-34.

Chapter 5

1. *Strong's Concordance,* H905, 19.

2. http://www.psychologytoday.com/blog/the-intelligent-divorce/ 201202/the-high-failure-rate-second-and-third-marriages.

3. http://www.ashastd.org/std-sti/std-statistics.html.

4. *Webster's Unabridged Dictionary,* 1453.

5. *Vines Expository* (Nashville: Thomas Nelson, 1997), 44-45.

Chapter 6

1. *Webster's Unabridged Dictionary,* 950.

2. Dwight Edwards, *Experiencing Christ Within* (Colorado Springs: Waterbrook Press, 2001), 5.

3. Ibid., 9.

4. Geoffrey W. Bromiley, *Theological Dictionary* (Grand Rapids, MI: Eerdmans, 1985), 481.

5. Pam Kanaly, *Will the Real Me Please Stand Up* (Mustang, OK: Tate, 2007), 224.

Chapter 7

1. Jerry Bridges, *The Bookends of the Christian Life* (Wheaton, IL: Crossway Books, 2009), 26.

2. *Strong's Concordance,* G4052, 1134.

3. Ibid., G714, 16.

4. Bridges, 5.

Chapter 8

1. Watchman Nee, *The Release of the Spirit* (Cloverdale, IN: Sure Foundation, 1965), 19.